The Making of Elizabethan
Foreign Policy, 1558–1603

UNA'S LECTURES

Una's Lectures, delivered annually on the Berkeley campus, memorialize Una Smith, who received her B.S. in History from Berkeley in 1911 and her M.A. in 1913. They express her esteem for the humanities in enlarging the scope of the individual mind. When appropriate, books deriving from the Una's Lectureship are published by the University of California Press:

1. *The Resources of Kind: Genre-Theory in the Renaissance*, by Rosalie L. Colie. 1973
2. *From the Poetry of Sumer: Creation, Glorification, Adoration*, by Samuel Noah Kramer. 1979
3. *The Making of Elizabethan Foreign Policy, 1558–1603*, by R. B. Wernham. 1980

R. B. WERNHAM

The Making of Elizabethan Foreign Policy, 1558–1603

UNIVERSITY OF CALIFORNIA PRESS

Berkeley   Los Angeles   London

University of California Press
Berkeley and Los Angeles, California
University of California Press, Ltd.
London, England
© *1980, by*
The Regents of the University of California

Printed in the United States of America

1   2   3   4   5   6   7   8   9

Library of Congress Cataloging in Publication Data
Wernham, Richard Bruce, 1906–
     The making of Elizabethan foreign policy, 1558–1603.
     (Una's lectures ; 3)
     Bibliography: p.
     Includes index.
     1.   Great Britain—Foreign relations—1485–1603. I. Title.   II. Series.
DA355.W39   327.42   80–10425
ISBN 0–520–03966–1
ISBN 0–520–03974–2 pbk.

Contents

Preface

The lectures of which this book is the printed version are here reproduced substantially as they were delivered at the University of California at Berkeley in April 1978. I have made a few minor additions and modifications to the text. I have added references for the quotations; but in an essay of this nature and scale it seemed unnecessary to cite portentously chapter and verse for every statement.

My thanks are due above all to Mr. Edward Hunter Ross and to the committee of the Una's Lectureship, to whose invitation these lectures and this book owe their existence. I must also thank my old friend, Professor Thomas Barnes, the chairman of the committee, for suggesting my subject and thereby giving me the opportunity and the incentive to look once again at Elizabethan foreign policy.

R. B. W.
Hill Head, Hants

I.

The Makers of Policy

In English foreign policy the reign of Queen Elizabeth I witnessed, I will not say a diplomatic revolution (historians have invented more than enough Tudor revolutions already), but at least a remarkable reversal of alliances. It was a reversal remarkable enough for Elizabethans themselves to remark upon it. Thus, in May 1589, less than a year after the defeat of Spain's "Invincible" Armada, Lord Burghley was commenting upon the strangeness of the alteration to his old friend, the Earl of Shrewsbury. "The state of the world," he wrote, "is marvellously changed when we true Englishmen have cause for our own quietness to wish good success to a French King and a King of Scots" and ill to a King of Spain.[1]

Strange indeed it was. After all, for close on five hundred years before Elizabeth I came to the throne, true Englishmen had been constantly wishing ill success to kings of France. Through most of the eighteenth century and much of the nineteenth, they would be doing so again. Yet during the century that followed Elizabeth's accession more and more of them came to regard France as more or less a friend and to feel that, as Oliver Cromwell told his second Parliament in 1656, "Truly your great enemy is the Spaniard: he is: he is a natural enemy."[2]

In this book we shall be concentrating particularly upon Anglo-

1. Lodge, *Illustrations of English History*, II.373.
2. T. Carlyle's *Letters and Speeches of Oliver Cromwell* (ed. S. C. Lomas), II.511.

Spanish relations and attempting to understand how the entente with Spain, first established by Henry VII through the treaty of Medina del Campo in 1489, came to break down in Elizabeth's time. We shall investigate how it was that during her reign this strange reversal of alliances came about; who and what caused that change of policy and national sentiment; and, briefly in conclusion, we shall touch upon some of its more significant long-term effects.

First, however, we should perhaps ascertain whether there was in fact any such thing as Elizabethan foreign *policy*. Or are we—as Professor Charles Wilson inclines to believe in his *Queen Elizabeth and the Revolt of the Netherlands*—are we simply "rationalising into policies, *ex post facto*, what was, in reality, a succession of shifts and muddles into which the Queen stumbled because she was so obsessed by understandable but irrational fears—the fear of rebellions, the fear of France especially—or the obverse of those fears—the deference towards Philip II [of Spain], the desire to recover Calais"?[3]

Irrational fear of rebellion? Irrational fear, in a Queen who might vaguely remember (she was three years old at the time) the Pilgrimage of Grace which had shaken her father's throne in 1536? who could well remember the risings which had brought down Protector Somerset in 1549? who could remember even better Wyatt's rebellion that so nearly brought down her sister Mary in 1554? who had herself to deal with the rebellion of the northern earls in 1569 and of the Earl of Essex in 1601, not to mention numerous Catholic assassination plots and Irish uprisings?

And *irrational* fear of France? Irrational fear, in a Queen who at her accession found the King of France "bestriding the realm, having one foot in Calais and the other in Scotland"[4] and with

3. C. Wilson, *Queen Elizabeth and the Revolt of the Netherlands*, p. 6.
4. "The Distresses of the Commonwealth" [1558], State Papers Domestic, i. no. 77.

his son and heir-apparent husband to the young Queen of Scots?

These, however, are secondary points. The crux of the matter is surely that any government's foreign policy is bound to consist largely of day-by-day responses, day-by-day reactions to the actions of all the other states with whom it has any sort of relationship. Those responses, those reactions, are normally determined primarily by what a government thinks or, no less often, by what it instinctively feels are its and the nation's essential interests. Assessments of what those essential interests are, and of their relative importance, will naturally vary to some extent from person to person; to some extent also according to the influence of different advisers and different pressure groups. But insofar as the responses spring from consistent and firm-seated instincts or from a clear and balanced appreciation of the true interests of the government and nation, they will in course of time build up into a coherent system, into something which we may fairly call a policy even though its initial responses were neither planned in advance nor seen as part of a systematic scheme. Generally speaking, it is only the very powerful or the very aggressive or the very doctrinaire who start out with a foreplanned policy. Yet even they are generally compelled to modify their plans in the face of the turns of fortune and the not always predictable reactions of their neighbors. A comparatively weak state, such as Elizabethan England was, cannot in its relations with mightier powers avoid feeling this compulsion even more strongly. However rational and consistent its aims, however clear and firm the *course* it sets, the actual *track* it follows must turn and twist this way and that, just as an Elizabethan galleon had to tack back and forth in response to winds and tides.

Now, Elizabeth was certainly a great twister and turner. But in saying that she merely stumbled into a succession of shifts and muddles I think Professor Wilson (like those older historians to whose attitude he reverts) fails to distinguish between the course she set and the track she had to follow. For surely what is truly remarkable about, for example, Elizabeth's policy towards the Netherlands from 1567 onward is her persistent pursuit by varied means of three steady purposes: to get the Spanish army out of the Netherlands; to prevent the French getting into the Netherlands; and to restore to the Netherlanders themselves, under continued Spanish protection, the ancient liberties and the measure of home rule that they had enjoyed under Philip II's father, the Emperor Charles V.[5] Other examples come easily to mind: her steady preference for an understanding with the French royal government rather than all-out support for the Huguenots; her consistent appreciation of the danger from the revived sea-power of Spain in the 1590s.

So, I think we can truly say that there *was* such a thing as Elizabethan foreign *policy*. Moreover, in its main lines it was clearly the foreign policy of Elizabeth herself. Of this it would be easy to multiply proofs; easy, but perhaps unnecessary, for it should be amply evidenced as we go along.

That the Queen should determine policy was, of course, natural enough in a state where the monarch ruled as well as reigned. For control of foreign policy, control over the dealings with fellow monarchs and governments, was the last thing any monarch would willingly give up. Not even George I or Louis XV was prepared to renounce his claim as it were to play in the World Series.

Besides, there was a very special reason why Elizabeth should want to keep personal control over her realm's foreign policy. During at least the first twenty or twenty-five years of her reign, it so often became entangled with the question of her own marriage and the question of the succession to her throne—the first a matter of some personal concern to herself; the second a matter of no less close concern to her subjects, who would still be there to rejoice or suffer after she herself was gone. So, with Elizabeth

5. R. B. Wernham, "English Policy and the Revolt of the Netherlands," in *Britain and the Netherlands* (ed. Bromley and Kossman), pp. 29–40.

it was not merely another case of "the buck stops here": in matters of foreign policy especially, she took unusually good care that it did not stop anywhere else.

This does not mean that Elizabeth's foreign policy was all her own work, that the ideas behind it sprung from her mind alone. As Professor MacCaffrey says in his study of *The Shaping of the Elizabethan Regime*: "The conception and initiation of policy was frequently left to the royal councillors; it became their business to devise the best possible mode of proceeding in each individual contingency of state. It remained for the Queen to accept, reject, or modify their proposals; there could be no question that the final decision remained a royal prerogative."[6] Or, as her younger contemporary Fulke Greville put it:

> Her Council Board (as an abridgement of all other jurisdictions) she held up in due honour, propounded not her great businesses of state to them with any prejudicate resolution which, once discovered, suppresseth the freedom both of spirit and judgement, but opens herself clearly, hears them with respect, observes number and reason in their voices and makes a quintessence of all their concords or discords within herself, whence the resolutions and directions came suddenly and secretly forth for execution.[7]

Most of the work was, of course, done by and through the Principal Secretary.[8] He (or they, for there were sometimes two of them) conducted the routine correspondence with ambassadors and agents, intelligencers and spies, soldiers abroad and sailors at sea. He also drafted the Queen's own letters for her approval and signature, while his clerks wrote the fair copies for despatch.

6. W. MacCaffrey, *The Shaping of the Elizabethan Regime*, p. 300.

7. Fulke Greville, *Life of Sir Philip Sidney* (ed. Nowell Smith, 1907), pp. 188–189.

8. F. M. G. Evans, *The Principal Secretary of State: A Survey of the Office from 1558 to 1680*.

But the Queen kept a close eye upon the Secretary's work. Let me give an example, one which also illustrates how difficult even an especially trusted councillor like Lord Burghley could find it even after many years in her close confidence, to persuade her to accept his counsel.

In November 1590 she sent Horatio Palavicino with a French ambassador, the Vicomte de Turenne, to Germany to hire an army to help Henry IV of France in fighting the Catholic League in France. The draft of Palavicino's open instructions forbade him to offer any contribution from the Queen toward this levy. Burghley, who was acting as Secretary during the vacancy of the office after Sir Francis Walsingham's death, persuaded her with much difficulty to add a secret clause, which even Turenne was not to be allowed to know about. This permitted Palavicino to offer up to £10,000 from her if he found the levy would not go forward without it. Then, in a final draft, Burghley inserted another secret clause allowing Palavicino to go up to £15,000 "in case of extreme necessity" and provided he first obtained written permission from the Queen. This clause Elizabeth promptly crossed out and only after further argument did she allow its reinstatement. After all, as she probably soon realized, Palavicino would still have to get her written permission for the extra £5,000—and it is significant that in fact he never dared to go above the £10,000.[9]

The Queen also kept a close watch upon incoming information. She expected ambassadors and agents, military and naval commanders, to write directly to her upon any matters of real importance. Most of them, it is true, wrote their regular, routine despatches to the Secretary or sometimes to the Privy Council. Thus, Sir Henry Unton during his first embassy to France wrote between late October 1591 and May 1592 sixty letters to Burghley (then acting as Secretary), seventeen to Sir Robert Cecil (who was

9. *List and Analysis of State Papers, Foreign Series* (ed. R. B. Wernham), II. paras. 753–758.

beginning to act as his father's assistant), seven to Sir Thomas Heneage, and only nine to the Queen. But those nine to the Queen contained full reports of such matters as his first audiences with Henry IV and his efforts to pacify Henry's unpaid and mutinous Germans (those same Germans toward whose levy Palavicino had paid out £10,000 of her money).[10]

It is true that Elizabeth did not conscientiously read all the incoming letters; that she found long despatches and long memoranda tedious; that she preferred hearing to reading when it came to state papers; and that the Secretary not infrequently found himself acting as a sort of verbal reader's digest. Yet there is ample evidence of the Queen's watchfulness in the large number of letters and documents among the foreign series of the State Papers that are endorsed with, or have their important passages indicated by, the trefoils marking them for her visual or aural attention.

Furthermore, of course, she could learn a good deal from the often quite lengthy audiences she gave to foreign ambassadors, particularly the resident ambassadors of France and, during the 1560s, of Spain. Her knowledge of languages, moreover, enabled her to conduct these audiences in the ambassador's own tongue or in Latin. Possibly, though, her French at least was—or became—a shade less proficient than her biographers would have us believe. For on two separate occasions, in 1590 and 1591, French ambassadors believed that she had promised to send their master troops, or at any rate the pay for troops, when she had certainly intended no such thing.[11] Perhaps, however, this was simply due to wishful hearing by the ambassadors.

In spite of Elizabeth's watchful control, the Principal Secretary obviously had considerable influence in the shaping of foreign policy and even more influence upon its carrying out. That was in part what he was there for. And it was especially true during

10. *Correspondence of Sir Henry Unton . . . in the years 1591 and 1592* (ed. J. Stevenson; Roxburghe Club).
11. *List and Analysis of State Papers, Foreign Series,* II. paras. 492, 540, 567.

the years between 1558 and 1572, when William Cecil was Secretary. The Secretary may have been rather less influential when between 1573 and 1590 Sir Francis Walsingham held the office, with brief assistance from, in turn, Sir Thomas Smith, Thomas Wilson, and (briefest of all) William Davison. Walsingham's influence was rather less than Cecil's had been because Cecil, now Baron Burghley and Lord Treasurer, was still usually consulted by Elizabeth on matters of foreign (as well, of course, as of domestic) policy, while most English ambassadors and agents, naval and military commanders, kept up almost as regular a correspondence with him as with Mr. Secretary Walsingham.

Dr. Conyers Read has traced in great detail, in five sizable volumes, how differences and rivalry over foreign policy developed between these two leading ministers during the 1570s and 1580s.[12] He has shown, too, how opinions in court and council about foreign affairs tended to polarize around them. During those years Walsingham, generally supported by the Queen's favorite the Earl of Leicester, pressed for the active and Protestant kind of foreign policy that Burghley had so often advocated in the 1560s; while Burghley, with advancing years and the cares of the Lord Treasureship upon his shoulders, grew more cautious and defensive as England itself grew under his and the Queen's nursing stronger and more independent.

It is tempting, therefore, to see Elizabeth's foreign policy, at least in the 1570s and 1580s, as the product of, and as run by, a sort of two-party system. It is all the easier to see it in this way because the information about it comes so largely from the State Papers, the archives of the Secretary now dispersed between the Public Record Office, the British Library, and Hatfield House. And these Elizabethan State Papers are so largely Cecil papers— the papers of William Cecil, Lord Burghley, and of his second

12. Conyers Read, *Mr. Secretary Cecil and Queen Elizabeth; Lord Burghley and Queen Elizabeth; Mr. Secretary Walsingham and the Policy of Queen Elizabeth* (3 vols.).

son Sir Robert Cecil, who became Secretary in 1596 after taking an increasing part in the Secretary's work following Walsingham's death in April 1590. To these Cecil papers were added most of Secretary Walsingham's papers which were brought into the new State Paper Office set up in James I's reign. To them were also added a good many of the papers of the Earl of Essex, acquired by Sir Robert Cecil after Essex's downfall. So discussions on foreign policy do appear all the more to polarize around Burghley and Walsingham in the 1570s and 1580s, and around the Cecils and Essex in the 1590s.

Now it seems likely that Elizabeth did rather more than just tolerate these rivalries. As Sir Robert Naunton, writing during the reign of Charles I, says, she "ruled much by faction and parties which she herself both made, upheld, and weakened as her own great judgement advised."[13] Most of the time, and particularly after the northern earls had been eliminated in 1569, these factions and parties, the struggle for power, position, profit, and patronage, centered (as Professor Elton has recently described)[14] upon the court. There the Queen could control it, could, indeed, use it to prevent any one minister or favorite from monopolizing the channels to her favor, to the rich rewards of power and position that lay in the monarch's gift.

This worked well until the last years of the reign, until in the 1590s the Earl of Essex broke the rules of the game and strove, like an Elizabethan Buckingham, to monopolize and coerce the royal favor, besides building up outside as well as inside the court a following among diplomats, officials, tenants, and, more dangerously, among soldiers and men of war. But more of that later: for at least until those last Essex-ridden years, Elizabeth was able to prevent any such hardening of the political arteries as would leave her at the mercy of two rival and rigid factions.

13. Sir Robert Naunton, *Fragmenta Regalia*, p. 4.
14. G. R. Elton, "Tudor Government: Points of Contact, III: The Court" in *Transactions of the Royal Historical Society*, XXVI. 211–228.

For until then what happened was that councillors and courtiers came together in loose, informal, largely *ad hoc* groups over particular issues. Then they broke up and re-formed into other groupings on other issues. Thus in October 1584 and again in March 1585 Burghley, supported by Archbishop Whitgift and Sir Walter Mildmay, appears to have opposed Leicester, Walsingham, and Hatton over the question of giving assistance to the Dutch. But it was also in that second half of 1584 that Burghley, Leicester, and Walsingham were opposing Whitgift and Hatton over the treatment of the English Puritans—it was in July that Burghley complained to Whitgift about the procedures of the Court of High Commission as "too much savouring of the Romish Inquisition."[15] And, indeed, even on foreign policy the differences between Burghley and Walsingham were almost as much about *when* and *how* as about *what* should be done.

Furthermore, although in matters of foreign policy Elizabeth during the 1570s and 1580s did mainly and normally consult with Burghley, Walsingham, and Leicester, these three did not entirely monopolize influence and counsel. Sometimes they were not even informed, let alone consulted. Thus, if Drake was telling the truth, Elizabeth took care that his plans in 1577 should not be known to Burghley. In the following year, at the height of the Anjou courtship, Leicester said that "our conference with Her Majesty about affairs is both seldom and slender."[16]

Her Majesty's formal consultations with her Privy Council as a body also tended to be seldom, though not slender. Sir John Neale has suggested that they were infrequent because she feared she might be overawed by the serried ranks of male chauvinism in her assembled Council.[17] That, however, I take leave to doubt.

15. *Calendar of State Papers, Foreign Series* (ed. S. C. Lomas), XIX.95–99; J. Strype, *Whitgift*, III.106; Conyers Read, *Lord Burghley and Queen Elizabeth*, pp. 306–313.

16. *The World Encompassed by Sir Francis Drake* (ed. W. S. W. Vaux), p. 204; *Relations politiques des Pays Bas* (ed. K. de Lettenhove), X.678.

17. J. E. Neale, *Queen Elizabeth*, pp. 74–75.

After all, within a very few weeks of her accession the Spanish ambassador wrote that "she gives her orders and has her way as absolutely as her father did,"[18] and thirty-odd years later, when the Earl of Essex, away in Normandy at the head of her troops there, received a sharply written royal reprimand, "he swooned often and did so swell that, casting himself upon his bed, all the buttons of his doublet brake away as though they had been cut with a knife."[19] No, it was the male councillors who trembled, not their Queen—they might well have said, as Bismarck did about interviews with Queen Victoria, "She makes me schweat."[20]

Nevertheless it was, as a rule, only at important junctures or when Elizabeth found decision unusually difficult that she consulted the full Privy Council. Thus she did so in December 1559, about intervening in Scotland;[21] again in June 1565, about the attitude to be adopted to the marriage of Mary, Queen of Scots, to the Earl of Darnley;[22] in October 1584 and March 1585, about helping the Dutch after the assassination of William the Silent;[23] or in August 1593, about withdrawing Sir John Norris and the English troops from Brittany after Henry IV's conversion to Roman Catholicism and his truce with the Catholic League.

Let me quote Burghley's report to Norris of that 1593 meeting. "Upon . . . reading of your letters," he wrote, "before Her Majesty and her Council hath grown this day much diversity of opinion, Her Majesty a great while utterly misliking your longer stay there" (for a number of reasons which Burghley summarized). However, "though Her Majesty held therefore those arguments of long time, yet upon arguments made by her Council to the contrary, she changed her opinion . . . and so in conclusion it was

---

18. *Calendar of State Papers, Spanish* (ed. M. A. S. Hume), I.7.
19. *List and Analysis of State Papers, Foreign Series*, III. para. 278.
20. J. Wheeler-Bennett, *Knaves, Fools, and Heroes*, p. 125.
21. *Calendar of State Papers, Foreign Series*, II. no. 483.
22. Ibid., VII.384–387.
23. Ibid., XIX.95–99; *Hist. MSS. Comm., Salisbury Papers*, III.67–70; Conyers Read, *Lord Burghley and Queen Elizabeth*, pp. 307–313.

advised that Her Majesty would continue her charge until the end of the truce."[24]

Although Elizabeth did not very frequently consult her Privy Council as a whole, she did make considerable use of small *ad hoc* committees of councillors, particularly for detailed negotiations with foreign ambassadors. Thus Burghley, Leicester, Walsingham, and Hatton carried on most of the negotiations with the Dutch envoys which resulted in the Treaty of Nonsuch in August 1585. Again, during the 1590s she frequently used two or three of her councillors to help Burghley when he was acting as Secretary after Walsingham's death. When she sent Thomas Wilkes on a special mission to the United Provinces in 1590, Burghley, Hatton, and Buckhurst jointly handled the correspondence with him. Burghley, too, once refused to open a letter addressed to the three of them until the other two were present.[25] In a less formal fashion, in 1591 Burghley, Hatton (till his death in December), Lord Admiral Howard, and Sir Thomas Heneage dealt with most of the correspondence with Essex in Normandy and with Sir Henry Unton during his first French embassy.

We get glimpses, too, of other councillors playing some part. For example, the Lord Keeper, Nicholas Bacon, had a good deal to say in those December 1559 discussions about Scotland;[26] so, too, had Sir Walter Mildmay in the debates of October 1584 about the Netherlands.[27] Incidentally, when Mildmay died in 1589 a spy he had sent to Italy, one Robert Allatt, reveals himself to us by writing to Burghley for instructions.[28] In the 1560s, again, it seems clear that the old Lord Treasurer, the Marquis of Winchester, was not without influence upon foreign policy; nor was the Earl of Sussex during the 1570s—but both these men

24. S. P. France (S.P.78), xxxii. fo. 83.
25. *List and Analysis of State Papers, Foreign Series,* II. para. 207.
26. *Calendar of State Papers, Foreign Series,* II. 197–198.
27. Ibid., XIX. 96.
28. *List and Analysis of State Papers, Foreign Series,* I. paras. 681–683.

lack good biographies. Sir James Croft, that "grey beard with a white head witless," as Lord Admiral Howard described him in his later years,[29] he, too, seems to have had some, less happy, influence. Less influentially, Sir Thomas Heneage had some part in secret service matters during the earlier 1590s: Châteaumartin, for example, addressed many of his intelligences from Bayonne jointly to Burghley and Heneage. None of these left papers, or at any rate any accumulation of papers. So here we are getting into a twilight area where we have to make the most of scraps and hints.

This is even more true when we look beyond the Privy Council and the privy councillors and try to see who else influenced or sought to influence the Queen's thinking and action in foreign affairs, in what ways, and to what degree. That there were such people is not in doubt. For example, in the earlier years of the reign Sir Nicholas Throckmorton wrote to her somewhat avuncular discourses on policy in general, besides seeking to guide her on particular issues by his despatches during his French and Scottish embassies. Then there was John Hawkins, who persuaded her to let him transform her navy from a coast-defense force into a high-seas fleet capable of operating at considerable distances from home—against the Spanish silver fleets from America, if he could persuade her to that. In later years there was Sir Walter Raleigh, with his plans for plantations in Ireland and America and his projects for winning the war against Spain. Neither he nor Throckmorton achieved their ambition to be Privy Councillor, yet their influence was not entirely negligible.

There were other men whose ambitions did not rise quite so high. There was that ebullient Welsh soldier Sir Roger Williams. In the war years he bombarded Queen and Council with advice (not always consistent advice) upon strategy; he once had the au-

29. *State Papers relating to the Defeat of the Spanish Armada* (ed. J. K. Laughton; Navy Records Society), I.49.

dacity to boast that Her Majesty could read his handwriting, which was more than he himself or anyone else could (or can) do![30] Then there were some of the higher "civil servants," especially those of course with diplomatic experience. Such a man was Henry Killigrew, Burghley's brother-in-law, who performed the rare feat of keeping in with both Burghley and Leicester. Killigrew was a Teller of the Exchequer who was frequently employed on diplomatic missions from the early 1560s until the 1590s. He was a man who thoroughly enjoyed a good deal of ill health and was perhaps too much of a "yes-man" to be very influential: as Field Marshal Haig said of the Earl of Derby, "Like the feather pillow, [he] bears the marks of the last person who has sat on him."[31] Nevertheless, he was much used and, on occasion, consulted. So, too, was Thomas Wilkes, a clerk of the Council, who was reckoned (and certainly reckoned himself) an expert on Netherlands affairs. On such matters he was quite often consulted by privy councillors such as Burghley, Walsingham, and Buckhurst, though by falling out with Leicester in 1587 he lost the Queen's favor for two or three years.

Besides these, there were the courtiers: some held court offices; others just hung around the court in the hope of preferment or pickings; others still merely visited the court periodically to keep in touch and to remind the Queen and her ministers of their existence. Among these we may put Sir Edward Stafford. In November 1589, after his return from his embassy to France, we find him accused of procuring unkindness in the Queen toward Henry IV by showing her a letter complaining that her troops were ill-used by the French.[32] Others we may mention are Henry, Baron Norris, and his wife, Elizabeth's much favored "Black

30. Sir Roger Williams to Burghley, 5 November 1592: S. P. France (S.P.78), xxix. fo. 286.

31. *The Private Papers of Douglas Haig, 1914–19* (ed. R. W. Blake), p. 279.

32. *List and Analysis of State Papers, Foreign Series*, I. para. 556.

Crow," who hatched a notable breed of Elizabethan soldiers. Their favor got Thomas Bodley into trouble when he was the resident in the United Provinces and took the Dutch States General's side against Sir Edward Norris, the governor of Ostend (and surely the fool of the family), who had misappropriated the States' revenues from the villages around Ostend.[33] This was, perhaps, hardly an example of influence upon high policy. Nevertheless, it did not make things easier for the eldest of the Norris brothers, Sir John, who was just at this moment trying to persuade the States to let him take away some of the Queen's troops in the Netherlands for service in Brittany.

Outside the court, as well as outside the Council, tbere were other influences that could make themselves felt upon the Queen's ministers, even when not directly upon the Queen herself. The centralization of England's overseas trade upon London, and the extent to which it was dominated by a small oligarchy of well-to-do London Merchant Adventurers, gave these men an opportunity to have a say in matters of foreign policy. Thus a list of notabilities who were to be consulted upon policy toward France, dated 25 May 1563, is headed by "the mayor of London and the aldermen."[34]

That the Queen should be open, in less or more degree, to these influences from outside her Privy Council resulted from the very nature of sixteenth-century English government at its upper, decision-making, level. At that level, court and Council, household and state were still very much interwoven. To use Bagehot's terms, the "dignified" and the "efficient" aspects of the monarchy very much overlapped, indeed, interlocked. The court, the ceremonial side, was wherever the Queen was. Except for a few summer weeks during the law courts' vacation, when she went on

33. Ibid., III. para. 137.
34. Quoted in G. D. Ramsay, *The City of London and International Politics at the accession of Elizabeth Tudor,* p. 77.

progress perhaps as far afield as Bath or Kenilworth or Southampton, even then not usually much more than seventy or eighty miles from London, the Queen was normally in one of her palaces near the capital. She would generally be at Greenwich or Richmond or Nonsuch or Windsor, even at Whitehall, in any case, within a fairly easy ride of the more settled abodes of the great departments of state and the central law courts at Westminster.

This meant that although the great officers of state—the Lord Chancellor, the Lord Treasurer, the Lord Admiral, the Principal Secretary, and the rest—could not always be at court, the Queen could still call any of them to her at a few hours' notice. And, not only them, but also lesser officials were equally within reach, besides, of course, the court and household officers, some of whom would always be in attendance. Thus it was easy for the Queen to take counsel with and to use any particular privy councillor or others not of the Privy Council. This also made it easier for her to ensure that however bureaucratic the Privy Council became in its administrative and executive capacity, it never became a policy-deciding cabinet.

All these contacts enabled the Queen, moreover, to get some idea of the wider fields of public opinion and national sentiment beyond her court and her Council. So, of course, did Parliament. But Parliaments met only about once every four years during her reign and then they rarely sat for more than a very few weeks. They, especially those of the later years, did number, among the Commons as well as the Lords, some members with knowledge and experience of foreign affairs: ex-ambassadors, soldiers, sailors, merchants trading overseas. They did on occasion express strong views on matters of foreign policy, as in urging the Queen's marriage and settlement of the succession in 1566; in pressing for the execution of Mary Stuart in 1572; in advocating more substantial aid to the Dutch and acceptance of the sovereignty over them in 1587.[35] Nevertheless, most of the members were better informed and more concerned about local and domestic affairs, and their occasional interventions about foreign policy were generally in the wake of agitation by the Privy Council or by some faction of privy councillors or officials. Parliaments were in any case too infrequent for their influence to be more than intermittent; and probably the Queen learned less about public opinion and national sentiment from them than from her councillors, courtiers, and "civil servants."

Many of these were interested, for example, in industrial and commercial ventures. Indeed, England's industrial and commercial progress during Elizabeth's reign owed a great deal to the interest and leadership of ministers and courtiers. Leicester invested in the nascent copper and brass industry, in the Muscovy Company, in the Morocco trade. Burghley had close contacts with the city and with leading Merchant Adventurers. Hatton backed Drake's 1577–1580 voyage around the world and Drake renamed his flagship, the *Pelican*, as the *Golden Hind*, which was Hatton's crest.

Besides such industrial and commercial connections, during at least the first two-thirds of the reign most councillors, officials, and courtiers had strong local roots in the country. It was not merely that so many preserved local links through their estates, as Burghley did at Theobalds in Hertfordshire and at Stamford in Lincolnshire; or through local offices as Lords Lieutenant, justices of the peace, rangers of forests, wardens of castles, even when some of such offices were executed by deputies. It was also that during the first thirty years of the reign—things were rather different in the 1590s—so many of them were actually recruited from the country, from outside the immediate court circle. Wal-

35. J. E. Neale, *Queen Elizabeth and Her Parliaments, 1559–81*, pp. 128–164, 247–290; *Queen Elizabeth and Her Parliaments, 1584–1601*, pp. 166–183.

singham, Raleigh, Hatton, Hawkins, Thomas Smith, William Davison, Thomas Bodley: none of these came from established court families, and the list could easily be multiplied.

This was the more important because the population of England was so small. It was probably under four million—the sixteenth century has some figures, but no statistics—even at the end of the reign. It was so small that, as Pickthorn has remarked, "There was hardly a county, and certainly not a town except perhaps London, where one man could not know, of his own direct knowledge, all that a government would care to ask about every inhabitant who was of any political or administrative importance."[36] And, of course, Council, court, the whole central bureaucracy were correspondingly small. They, too, were few enough for the Queen to know of *her* own direct knowledge every one of *them* who was of political or administrative importance.

A further consequence of the close interconnection between court and Council, between household and state, was that a great deal of what was discussed and decided at these upper levels of government was discussed and decided and done by word of mouth, and thus left only occasional and scattered written records. Nor were all the gaps filled by the archive of the Principal Secretary. For another peculiarity of the Elizabethan State Papers is that, while they tell us a great deal in very considerable detail about the execution of foreign policy and about routine diplomatic and military matters, they tell us a great deal less about the actual making of policy.

We do, of course, get occasional insights, for example, in the notes of those debates of December 1559, June 1565, and October 1584, or in those drafts of Palavicino's instructions in November 1590. Sometimes, too, we can learn a good deal from what a Secretary or a privy councillor or even the Queen herself wrote to ambassadors or commanders. Witness the Queen's sharp rep-

36. K. Pickthorn, *Early Tudor Government*, I.68.

rimands to Sir John Norris and Sir Francis Drake in Portugal in 1589 for ignoring her instructions,[37] or that account which Burghley sent to Norris in 1593 of the Queen and Privy Council's discussions about withdrawing her forces from Brittany. Nevertheless, Secretaries and privy councillors were often chary of opening their minds too freely to these subordinates. Thus Secretary Cecil's letters to Sir Nicholas Throckmorton in France in the early 1560s became steadily less revealing. Again, in the 1580s Secretary Walsingham usually picked his words carefully in writing to a later ambassador in France, Sir Edward Stafford, whom he did not greatly trust and who was moreover Burghley's man.

Moreover, in the very nature of things and with even the most industrious of Secretaries, the number of letters going out was bound to be far less than the number of letters coming in. And this was a disparity that is exaggerated in the surviving State Papers by the practice of the Elizabethan Secretary's office. For, apart from the Signet Clerks who handled the more formal, sealing, side of the work, the Secretary's office was probably the least bureaucratic in the central administration. Its clerks were the personal servants of the Secretary, not direct employees of the Crown. They came in and went out with the Secretary. Among them there does not seem to have been any very hard and fast formal division of duties, though no doubt there were private, informal, perhaps temporary, arrangements. And certainly no one of them was specifically a keeper of records. It was not until James I's reign that a Keeper of the State Papers was established.

So the survival of the Elizabethan Secretary's archives, of the Elizabethan State Papers, is the result rather of failure to destroy than of any very positive purpose to preserve. A corollary of this was that little systematic effort was made to record the letters sent out of, or the papers, memoranda, etc., made in the office. There

37. S. P. Domestic, ccxxiv. no. 53.

are one or two letter books from the later years of the reign (they are a bit of a puzzle), but there is no regular, systematic series of entry books of out-letters until 1660. There is nothing corresponding to the medieval Chancery's series of Close Rolls.

What is preserved in the way of out-letters therefore consists of a lot of miscellaneous, chance-preserved papers. There are corrected drafts—sometimes so heavily corrected that historians have mistaken their messiness for incoherence, as with the instructions to Norris and Drake for the Portugal expedition of 1589.[38] There are fair copies of documents that were never issued; for example, instructions for Buckhurst to go on a mission to the Dutch in 1590,[39] which misled the *Dictionary of National Biography* into saying that he went. There are various odd papers, such as the letter that Elizabeth had begun to sign, "but misliking the great writing of her pen, she forebore the signing of this and signed another new written"; or the letter to the Dutch States General that she signed as "votre bonne cousine" instead of as "votre bonne bien amie," and that had therefore also to be re-written.[40]

Now this all means that the great majority of the Elizabethan State Papers are in-letters, letters received rather than letters sent out. Hence they give—to put it in military terms—very largely one-front, one theater-of-operations, local views. They show considerably less of the overall situation as it might appear to a supreme commander who had to look at strategy and policy as a whole, on all fronts. Thus we find Lord Willoughby early in 1589, bitterly bemoaning the disasters he feared must befall in the Netherlands if any of his troops were withdrawn for the Portugal expedition. Yet a few months later there is Norris in Portugal urging that all the English troops in the Low Countries should

38. Ibid., ccxxii. no. 89.
39. S. P. Holland (S.P. 84), xxxv. fos. 349–354.
40. Ibid., fo. 100; xxxviii. fo. 88.

be sent to reinforce him.[41] Or, again, we find Sir Roger Williams repeatedly urging that all of the war effort should be concentrated, now in Portugal, now in Brittany, now in Normandy—wherever, in fact, he happened to be serving at the time he wrote.

The effects of this one-sidedness in the State Papers are considerable. I suspect that this stream of more or less alarming news from foreign parts tended to make the Secretary, especially perhaps Walsingham, more nervous and jumpy than other privy councillors. We have, for example, already noted the change in Burghley's attitude when he changed from being Principal Secretary to being Lord Treasurer. The effects of this lop-sidedness in the Elizabethan State Papers, which nevertheless remain the principal source for the study of Elizabethan foreign policy, upon historians from James Anthony Froude onward has been equally noticeable. They have all too often followed the grumbles and anxieties of the local commanders or the local ambassadors and done less than justice to the wider and more balanced view that the Queen had to take.

Now this may be beginning to sound as if, even though Elizabeth did have a foreign policy, it is nearly impossible to discover just how it was made. That, however, would at this early stage be an unduly pessimistic conclusion. Nevertheless it is true that we often have to judge Elizabethan foreign policy and how it was made as much by what was done or attempted as by reasons recorded in writing. This is especially true in assessing the weight to be given to ideas and interests outside the Privy Council and the court circle, in particular to those of overseas trade and to those of religion. Trade, and, indeed, religion too were certainly controlled in the interests of national policy and not national policy in the interests of trade or even of religion.

Nevertheless, national policy itself was shaped quite as much

41. *Calendar of State Papers, Foreign Series*, XXIII.36–38, 53–55; S. P. Domestic, ccxxiv. no. 22.

by circumstances as by the will of the Queen or the persuasions of her privy councillors or the interests of commerce or the pressures of religion. For, as Sir Edward Grey, the British Foreign Secretary in 1914, once wrote: "There is in great affairs so much more, as a rule, in the minds of the events (if such an expression may be used) than in the minds of the chief actors."[42]

42. Grey of Falloden, *Twenty-Five Years, 1892–1916*, I.51.

II.

The First Quarrels with Spain

Having seen something of the makers of the Elizabethan foreign policy, let us now look at the origins and growth of the first quarrels between Elizabethan England and Spain, the quarrels that developed during the 1560s and early 1570s. These quarrels are good examples of what Sir Edward Grey meant by there being often "so much more, as a rule, in the minds of the events . . . than in the minds of the chief actors." For they were not primarily due to deliberately hostile policies on the part of either government, or at least of either sovereign. They were the outcome partly of Elizabeth's efforts to reassert England's independence, partly of Philip II's determination to reassert his authority against the opposition, and eventual rebellion, in his Netherlands provinces.

During the decade before Elizabeth's accession, England had twice been in serious danger of losing her independence. The country was in the sixteenth century a middleweight, at best, in a world dominated by two heavyweights, Spain and France. The King of Spain at this time ruled also over the Netherlands, Franche-Comté, much of Italy, and the Spanish settlements in the Americas. The population of Spain alone was probably two or three times as great as that of England. King Philip II's income was even more disparate, especially now that the great silver

Spain, France and the British Isles

The King of Spain's Territories

The King of Spain's Clients

Scot-
land

Ireland

North Sea

ENGLAND

N

W   E

S

Scilly Isles

Netherlands

Lorraine

Franche-Comté

Parma
Modena

Switzerland

FRANCE

Savoy

Milan

Venice

Portugal

Genoa
Tuscany

SPAIN

Corsica

Papal
States

Naples

Sardinia

Mediterranean
Sea

Sicily

Morocco

Algeria

Tunis

mines at Potosí in South America were coming on stream so that, as Sir Roger Williams put it a few years later, "His treasure comes unto him as our salads to us; when we have eat all, we fetch more out of our gardens. So doth he fetch his treasure out of the ground after spending all that is coined."[1]

France, the other heavyweight, had a population at least three or four times as great as England's and threatened a greater, because a nearer, danger than Spain. For, having just snatched Calais from Mary Tudor, France now possessed the entire southern, windward shore of the Channel. This was a considerable advantage when ships could not sail close to the wind and the prevailing southerly and westerly winds might pen the English navy in port for days or even weeks. Moreover, France, through its fast-growing domination over its old ally Scotland, had access through England's "postern gate" across England's only land frontier. This was particularly dangerous when Elizabeth came to the English throne, because Scotland's young queen, Mary Stuart, was married to the French king's son and heir. She was also, although statutorily barred, genealogically heir-presumptive to the Crown of England. She was, indeed, in many Roman Catholic eyes, rightful present Queen of England instead of the heretic Elizabeth, whose father's and mother's marriage had been pronounced unlawful by the Pope.

This last point was the more serious because both Spain and France were officially Roman Catholic and both their Kings were becoming gravely alarmed by the spread of heresy in their realms and by the challenge it, particularly in its Calvinist form, was beginning to make to their political authority. Could England under a Protestant or at any rate a not-Catholic, queen therefore still rely, as she had relied during the first half of the century, upon the secular jealousy between these two Roman Catholic superpowers to drive one to support her if the other turned hos-

1. *List and Analysis of State Papers, Foreign Series,* II. para. 467.

tile? Might they not be induced by the exhortations of a revitalized and aggressive Papacy to turn their combined arms against this country that was again slipping out of the Papal fold?

There was one encouraging circumstance. After half a century of wars, fought mostly in Italy, both France and Spain were financially and psychologically exhausted. Neither, therefore, was prepared to risk the renewal of general war over the British Isles. And, as both knew, aggression against England by either one of them could hardly be tolerated by the other. For England was of great, indeed of vital, importance to both of them. If it fell under French control, as it had so nearly done in the last year or two of Edward VI's reign, that would go far toward cutting off the Netherlands from Spain and would deal a serious, if not a fatal, blow to Spanish greatness. If it fell under Spanish control, as it had done even more recently through Mary Tudor's marriage to Philip II, that would go far toward cutting French communications with Scotland. More serious still, it would all but close that throttling ring of Spanish territories and dependencies that encircled France from the Pyrenees along the western Alps through Franche-Comté and the Netherlands. Add to this that England possessed a regular war navy, something which was unparalleled in Spain or France; a navy, too, backed by an equally unparalleled regular administrative service. True, the navy was small and somewhat run-down and its administration not free from corruption. Nevertheless, it was still a force to be reckoned with, as foreign observers recognized.

During the decade before Elizabeth's accession much else besides the navy had been allowed to run down, and England's weakness and disunity had made it seem, in Paget's phrase, "a bone between two dogs."[2] Determination to end this situation, to reassert England's independence, was the main driving-force be-

2. *Calendar of State Papers, Foreign Series*, II.3.

hind the policies of Elizabeth and her ministers, of William Cecil especially. This was so not only in their foreign policy, but in every aspect of affairs. It inspired the government's efforts to develop new industries, and to encourage old industries, that would make the country no longer dependent upon imports from abroad for firearms, artillery, gunpowder, copper wire for wool carding, and other necessities of defense and subsistence. It underlay the Queen's efforts to restore unity, or at least to damp down dissension in ecclesiastical matters while again breaking with Rome.

In foreign affairs during the first half of the 1560s this same determination to reassert England's independence found expression in hostility to France rather than to Spain. The first step was to put an end to French domination in Scotland by supporting, secretly at first, then openly in arms, the Protestant and nationalist revolt there in 1559–1560. It was a terribly risky but skillfully timed and ultimately successful intervention, though in its final stages fumblingly executed by the troops sent in to assist the Scots in expelling the French soldiery. For its success, and indeed for its inception, much of the credit must go to William Cecil; for the skillfulness of its timing the Queen herself was largely responsible.

This was followed in 1562–1564 by a superficially similar armed intervention on the side of the Huguenots in the first of sixteenth-century France's numerous "Wars of Religion." This intervention, largely inspired by Robert Dudley the Queen's favorite, soon to be made Earl of Leicester, ended in disaster. The English army sent over to Normandy, less to assist the Huguenots than to hold Le Havre as a bargaining counter for the recovery of Calais, was forced to surrender when the Huguenots remembered belatedly that they were Frenchmen and turned to bite the English hand that had been stretched out ostensibly to help them. It was an object lesson in the unreliability of foreign Protestant rebels that Elizabeth was never to forget. Nevertheless, it was not without its beneficial fruits. For when once peace was restored in 1564 the French royal government—at least so long as the Queen Mother Catherine de Medici had influence in it—made it a guiding principle thenceforward to maintain friendship with England, even if this meant abandoning Mary Stuart and hopes of French domination in Scotland.

This taming of French hostility and winning of Scottish amity were fundamental achievements. England need now no longer fear a Franco-Scottish stab in the back through the "postern gate," no longer would face the probability of a war on two fronts if relations with France again deteriorated. For all practical purposes England became an island. Invasion now could only be sea-borne, the kind that the country was least ill-equipped to deal with, as Henry VIII had demonstrated in 1545.

Nevertheless, while Scottish amity was being won and French hostility was being tamed, Spanish friendship was cooling. Philip II was probably more relieved than grieved by Elizabeth's polite rejection of his offer of marriage. Certainly he made the offer with no great enthusiasm. "Such a marriage," he wrote to his ambassador at Elizabeth's court, "would appear like entering upon a perpetual war with France, seeing the claims that the Queen of Scots has to the English throne."[3] It would be ruinously expensive, too. Nevertheless, "I have decided to place on one side all other considerations which might be urged against it and am resolved to render this service to God and offer to marry the Queen of England," provided, of course, that she professed the Roman Catholic faith. This was no way to propose to a proud and vain young woman of twenty-five; but doubtless Philip half hoped to have his suit rejected.

All the same, one who took his title of Most Catholic King as seriously as Philip did could hardly fail to be distressed to see

3. *Calendar of State Papers, Spanish*, I.21–23.

Elizabeth acting so vigorously and so often as Defender of what to him was altogether the wrong Faith. It was bad enough that in England itself Roman Catholicism was falling into near-fatal decline, as the government damped down the religious temperature and as the old Catholic priests died off with none as yet to replace them. It was worse that Elizabeth was actively encouraging Protestant rebels in Scotland and France and maybe even in Philip's own Netherlands, however much she might protest that she was merely upholding Scottish liberties against French encroachments, or intervening in France to regain Calais rather than to assist the Huguenots.

Yet what worried the Spaniards in these early years was not only, was not even chiefly, that Elizabeth was supporting the wrong religion. What most worried them was that she was taking such seemingly appalling risks in confronting the power of France. It made them fear that they might be drawn into another long and exhausting war to bail the English out. They had nothing but contempt for England's military strength. Indeed, as Cecil recognized, in military matters the country had hardly as yet emerged from the bow-and-arrow stage. The modernizing and re-equipping of England's land forces was to be one of the important Elizabethan achievements, but it was an achievement of the 1570s and 1580s. In the 1560s the country had only antiquated and ill-armed levies to put against the fire-power of France's military forces. And for Spain, a French Great Britain would be even worse than a Protestant Great Britain.

Philip did what he could to lessen these dangers. He persuaded the Pope to withhold his excommunication of Elizabeth. He tried to persuade Elizabeth herself to act more circumspectly. But he would not risk a renewal of war with France by using force to compel the English Queen to proceed more discreetly. Not all his ministers, however, shared Philip's patience. Some, like his first ambassador to Elizabeth, the Count of Feria, felt that En-

gland was "more fit to be dealt with sword in hand than by cajol-
ery."[4] This view was shared by Cardinal Granvelle, Philip's chief
minister with the Regent Margaret of Parma in the Netherlands.
Granvelle had special reasons for impatience. He was convinced
that English merchants at Bruges and Antwerp were aiding and
encouraging the growing Calvinist minority in the Low Countries. He suspected, too, that the English government might
not only be encouraging the Calvinists but also be abetting the
mounting opposition that he was encountering from the Netherlands nobility—from William of Orange, the Count of Egmont,
Count Horne, and the rest. Elizabeth's interventions to aid the
Lords of the Congregation in Scotland in 1560 and to aid the
French Huguenots in 1562 therefore took on, in Granvelle's
mind, the appearance of an international Protestant conspiracy
that had the Netherlands next on its list.

Granvelle's anger was brought to boiling point by Elizabeth's
licensing of a general privateering war against French Catholics
at sea in 1563. This added solid Netherlands and Spanish grievances to the Cardinal's suspicions and to the grievances already
felt by certain sections of the Netherlands business world over the
very considerable increases in English customs duties by the new
1558 Book of Rates and over older and more long-disputed dues.
The Channel and Narrow Seas were soon swarming with English
and Huguenot privateers who made little distinction between
French Catholic and other Catholic shipping—and the richest
and most numerous Catholic shipping in the Channel was Netherlands and Spanish. These privateers thus became a serious nui-
sance, indeed a considerable menace, to Spanish and Netherlands trade and communications.

Then, toward the end of 1563, Granvelle got his chance. That
autumn the English troops, returning from the disaster at Le
Havre, brought the plague to London and southeastern England.

4. Ibid., p. 3.

In November Granvelle, seizing upon the plague as a pretext, placed an embargo on all cloth imports from London. Elizabeth retaliated, and soon Anglo-Netherlands trade was at a standstill.

Granvelle was confident that the stoppage must soon bring the English government to its knees. After all, no trade meant no customs duties and the customs were, with the land revenues, one of the two great pillars of English crown finance. Besides, at least three-quarters of all England's overseas trade passed through London to Antwerp and the Low Countries. This excessive concentration, putting so many eggs into the one basket, was dangerous enough in itself. What made it doubly dangerous was that well over three-quarters of all English exports were cloth, woollen cloth. For the cloth manufacture was the only considerable industry in what was still an overwhelmingly agricultural country. Now, as something like one-half of the total English production of cloth was exported, and as all that cloth was woollen cloth, a slump or stoppage in exports affected not only the spinners, weavers, and others who made up the cloth but also the farmers and landowners whose sheep grew the wool.

This excessive concentration of England's overseas trade upon Antwerp was a matter that had been worrying English governments and some of the English Merchant Adventurers ever since, in 1550, Antwerp had for the first time been glutted, had for the first time been unable to dispose of all the cloth the English merchants brought over for sale. Under Northumberland, and under Mary, too, there had been sporadic attempts to find other outlets, other "vents" to use the Elizabethan word, for English exports and other sources for English imports. For such purposes the Muscovy Company, trading to Russia through the White Sea, had been established in 1553, and Wyndham had made his West African voyage in the same year. Elizabeth's government, too, in its anxiety to reassert England's independence, had already given the problem some thought. The first of John Hawkins's West African–West Indian voyages in 1563 was, in a sense, an extension of the Wyndham enterprises. Even earlier than that, back in April 1560, Cecil had been wondering "How the vent of cloths might be issued unto the Holst [i.e., Holstein] or other places."[5] The sharpening quarrel with the Hanseatic Towns, however, over the restriction of their trading privileges in England—another aspect of the reassertion of English independence—made it difficult to find a new "vent" in Germany.

Granvelle's 1563 embargo gave the matter a fresh urgency. So in 1564 the English government negotiated an agreement with Emden whereby the Merchant Adventurers transferred their trade from Antwerp thither. As Emden lay just outside the Netherlands, the Merchant Adventurers were also granted a new charter which extended their monopoly to include northwestern Germany. The new charter also strengthened their control over the trade, and by strengthening the oligarchical character of their organization, incidentally made it easier for the government to direct and control them.

Nevertheless, although Cecil had probably been in touch with Emden eight months before the Granvelle embargo, the move there was something of an improvisation. "It fell out upon a casualty," as Cecil put it. At this stage, even he was not going beyond thinking how good it would be "to divert *some part* of our trade"[6] away from Antwerp. That, however, was still further than many, both in the merchant community and in government and court circles, were as yet ready to go. This was particularly true among the smaller traders, for to them the great attraction of the Antwerp trade was that it required only a small capital. It could be, and was, carried in quite small ships—few used in that traffic were above fifty, or at the outside eighty, tons. Small ships needed only small crews and the short passage across the Narrow Seas meant that little of the cargo space would be filled with their

5. Quoted in Conyers Read, *Mr. Secretary Cecil and Queen Elizabeth*, p. 167.

6. T. Wright, *Queen Elizabeth and Her Times*, I.175.

victuals. Nor for that brief journey was much armament necessary. So, as soon as a settlement was patched up with the Netherlands government in December 1564 (after Granvelle's dismissal) and as trade was reopened in January 1565, the Merchant Adventurers flocked back to Antwerp, for which Emden had indeed proved but a poor substitute.

Nor was it only the Merchant Adventurers who were loth to see the Antwerp connection broken or seriously reduced. Sir Thomas Smith (the author of *De Republica Anglorum*, Principal Secretary under Edward VI and again in 1572, who was now, in 1565, the resident English ambassador in France) regarded Anglo-Netherlands trade as a guarantee of Anglo-Spanish friendship. He believed that because of their English trade the Netherlands could "by no provocation be brought to have war with England six months together." Had they not compelled Charles V to let them opt out of his quarrel with Wolsey's England in 1528 precisely six months after the outbreak of that conflict? So, Smith went on, "I may call the peace with France one of discretion, with Flanders and Brabant one of necessity"[7]—of necessity to both England and Spain. Smith's views were widely shared, and not only among the more conservative nobility, such as the Howards, or among the Catholic or semi-Catholic nobles and gentry such as the northern Earls of Westmorland and Northumberland, who were growing increasingly alarmed at the steady decline of the old religion and the progress of Protestantism at home as well as abroad. Many besides these, many moderate men and Protestants, still felt that England needed Spanish friendship if it was not to be at the mercy of the old enemy France, and that Spanish friendship went with the Antwerp trade.

During the next few years, however, the mounting opposition to Spanish rule in the Netherlands and the increasing distur-

7. Quoted in Conyers Read, *Mr. Secretary Cecil and Queen Elizabeth*, p. 295.

bances that culminated in the widespread image-breaking and desecration of Catholic churches during the riots of the summer of 1566 cast more and more doubts upon Antwerp's adequacy as an international trading center. The doubts afflicted Italians and Germans and Portuguese as well as Englishmen and they made the English Merchant Adventurers less unready to consider moving. So, in May 1567 an agreement was made with Hamburg, despite the ill will and opposition of the other Hanse Towns. By this agreement the Merchant Adventurers were to transfer their trade to Hamburg, where they were promised special privileges and accommodation for the next ten years. Now, Hamburg was probably the one place in northwestern Europe that could provide a real alternative "vent," and not just a trickling overflow, to Antwerp. So a move there must greatly diminish, if it did not entirely end, England's dependence upon Spain and the Spanish Netherlands in matters of trade and finance. And the events of the next eighteen months ensured that the move took place.

The first of those events happened barely three months after the English agreement with Hamburg. In August 1567 the Duke of Alba marched into Brussels at the head of 10,000 Spanish troops to stamp out the already dying embers of the 1566 conflagration. He was soon reinforced by Italian, German, and Walloon levies to over 50,000 men. Thereupon the hitherto largely home-ruling and militarily inoffensive Netherlands became the garrison area of the biggest and best army in Christendom.

This was one of the great turning points of early modern history. The Netherlands westward frontier lay a bare ninety miles from Paris; its westward coast lay little more than thirty miles from the coast of Kent, little more than a hundred miles from the Thames estuary and London. For both France and England, therefore, the presence of this great Spanish army, this shifting northward of the center of gravity of Spanish military power, was a matter of urgent concern. Indeed, for the next hundred years, until the final collapse of Spanish power in the Netherlands in the 1667 War of Devolution, two of the dominant themes of western European international relations would be Spain's anxiety to keep open the communications with its main army in the Low Countries, and French determination to sever those communications.

For the moment, however, from September 1567 until September 1570, France was rendered helpless by civil wars. The Huguenots rose in rebellion, suspecting, wrongly, that the levies of Swiss troops made by their government to watch Alba's march from Italy were intended against themselves, were, in fact, the first-fruits of the Roman Catholic conspiracy they suspected Alba and Catherine de Medici had hatched in a meeting at Bayonne back in 1565. So Philip II had, for the time being, little or nothing to fear from France—all the less because the downfall of Mary Stuart in Scotland in June 1567 dealt what was almost the final blow to French hopes of dominant influence there.

How, then, would Philip employ Alba's great army when once the Netherlands were subdued? Would he take advantage of French impotence to bring England back by force to the Papal and Habsburg fold? Certainly that was what Cecil and a good many other English privy councillors feared, and some of Philip's actions encouraged those fears. In the spring of 1568 he brusquely expelled from his court the resident English ambassador, Dr. John Mann. This was, in fact, hardly surprising, for Dr. Mann was, to begin with, an odd choice as ambassador to Catholic Spain—a married Protestant cleric, who had been Warden of Merton College, Oxford, and was now Dean of Gloucester. His behavior, moreover, even if pardonable in an academic, was less than tactful in an ambassador. An ambassador in Madrid just did not at his dinner table call the Pope "a canting little monk."[8] All the same, Mann's expulsion looked sinister to nervous Englishmen, the more so because in September of the same year Philip

---

8. *Calendar of State Papers, Spanish,* II.29.

recalled his own resident ambassador from England, the friendly de Silva, and replaced him by the notoriously hawkish Guerau de Spes, a crony of the Duke of Feria and of the English Catholic exiles.[9] This, again, had a fairly innocuous explanation. De Silva had been four years in his job, which was about as long as most ambassadors' finances could manage, and he had been begging for a change. Nevertheless, these actions of Philip's were not re-assuring.

Yet when William of Orange in this same summer of 1568 invaded the Netherlands in an attempt to raise a revolt that would drive out Alba, the English government made no move to assist him. The reason was that even Cecil, the councillor most alive to the potential threat of Alba's army, realized that any serious, official aid to William might well mean war with Spain. That was a war that England was still very ill-prepared to face. More-over, it would be a single-handed war, since France would be unable to help and an exploratory mission to Germany by Henry Killigrew made it clear that very few of the Protestant princes there were prepared to challenge Habsburg power. Besides, ex-perience in Scotland in 1560 and even more in France in 1562–1563 had taught Cecil, and still more sharply Elizabeth, how little reliance could be placed upon foreign Protestant rebels.

Nevertheless, although by the autumn of 1568 Alba had run William of Orange out of the Netherlands, his troubles were not yet all over. His mastery over the country depended upon his army; his control over his army depended upon his ability to pay it; and William's invasion had spoiled his hope of doing that and in addition sending "a river of silver" back to Spain. He had, on the contrary, to ask Philip to send *him* money. Philip, faced with a serious rebellion of the Moriscos in Spain and with a growing Turkish threat to the western Mediterranean—they had besieged

9. Guerau de Spes's embassy has been studied in the unpublished Oxford D.Phil. thesis (1972) by J. Retamal Favreau.

Malta in 1565—was also short of money and had to borrow from the bankers of Genoa to meet Alba's need. The loan, some £80,000, was sent round in specie from Spain aboard five small unarmed ships. Bad weather and Huguenot privateers forced them to seek shelter, some in Plymouth and one in Southampton. De Spes, newly arrived in England, thereupon asked Elizabeth to see the money safely conveyed, by sea or overland, to Flanders.

At first Elizabeth seemed ready to do this, and as late as 18 December 1568 de Spes wrote to assure Philip that the prospects seemed fairly good.[10] The money was, however, unloaded and brought ashore—for safety, it was said. Cecil also had discovered that until it was handed over at Antwerp it still legally belonged to the Genoese bankers, who might be ready to lend it to Elizabeth instead of to Philip. He mentioned this question of ownership to de Spes on December 21 and de Spes jumped to the (perhaps slightly premature) conclusion that Elizabeth had decided to seize the money. He wrote off at once to warn Alba and to suggest that the Duke should order the counter-seizure of English ships and goods in the Netherlands and Spain.[11] This Alba promptly did, on December 28—before he knew that on December 29 Elizabeth had told de Spes definitely that she was indeed taking over the loan.[12] News of Alba's action reached London on January 3 and Elizabeth immediately retaliated in kind. It was 1563–1564 over again.

Why did Elizabeth and Cecil indulge in what Professor Wilson calls "an escapade as costly as it was senseless"?[13] Costly, perhaps, it was, but was it entirely senseless? Why did they do it? I must confess that I find it difficult to be as dogmatic on this point as Professor Wilson. Elizabeth herself was certainly short of money

10. *Calendar of State Papers, Spanish*, II.88.
11. Ibid., p. 92.
12. *Relations politiques des Pays Bas* (ed. K. de Lettenhove), V.205.
13. C. Wilson, *Queen Elizabeth and the Revolt of the Netherlands*, p. 26.

and the Netherlands disturbances, followed by Alba's rule, had made it almost impossible to borrow in the former fashion at Antwerp—that was why Philip had to borrow in Genoa. It seems highly probable, too, that as Dr. Conyers Read suggests, Elizabeth and Cecil had not expected so fierce a reaction from Alba.[14] Possibly, as he also suggests, their idea was to hold the money while bargaining over rewards for its salvage. And of course, the 1496 Intercursus Magnus and other Anglo-Netherlands treaties did require that no reprisals should be made until after a formal protest and refusal of justice. So Alba, by his precipitate action, had put himself legally in the wrong.

Alba's reaction was, indeed, significant. Realizing that he had been hustled into hostile action prematurely by de Spes, he quickly sent an envoy to England to patch things up. This gave Elizabeth and Cecil the chance and the confidence to draw the matter out at length. When we remember Cecil's, and to some extent Elizabeth's, earlier alarm over the presence of the Spanish army in the Netherlands, it does seem at least plausible to suspect that in thus dragging out the negotiations they were not entirely innocent of ideas about making life difficult for Alba. And if now, why not in originally seizing the Genoese loan?

And surely they did make life difficult for him. It is true that the loan was less than a fifth of the annual cost of his army. But it was the crucial fifth, like the sixpence in Mr. Micawber's famous equation. The proof of this lies not only in the rapidity of Alba's attempt to open negotiations with Elizabeth. It is even more obvious in the hastening of his attempt to impose, as early as March 1569, a new system of permanent taxes on the Netherlands, the notorious Tenth and Twentieth Penny sales taxes. This attempt provoked such an outcry, even from his own councillors, that he had to postpone the plan for two years in return for grants of the traditional sort, wrung from the provincial estates only after

14. Conyers Read, *Mr. Secretary Cecil and Queen Elizabeth*, p. 433.

considerable bullying. The harm done went deeper still, as appeared when the next rebellion came in 1572. Then the burghers of Holland and Zeeland would refuse, as those of Gouda put it, to fight for Alba and the Tenth Penny even against the wild Sea Beggars and such "hirsute and savage corsairs" (the description is Motley's)[15] as the Count de la Marck.

Nevertheless, this quarrel over the seizure of the Genoese loan did make life difficult for Elizabeth and Cecil too. For in 1569 there were plenty of Englishmen, merchants and nobles, at court and in the country, who, as in 1563–1564, felt that Spain's friendship was essential for England's safety and that Spain's friendship went with the Antwerp trade. As a result, a formidable get-rid-of-Cecil movement quickly developed. It grew, not just among northern Catholics, conservative Howards, and such like. Many moderate men, non-Catholics, actual Protestants, jumped onto the anti-Cecil bandwagon, men like the Earl of Pembroke, the Earl of Sussex, even the Earl of Leicester. They had the sympathy of many London and East Coast merchants and businessmen, worried over the trade stoppages.

The movement was reinforced by the growing, widespread anxiety among all classes and all shades of religion about the succession to the throne, and by mounting exasperation over Elizabeth's repeated evasions of growing pressure from Privy Council, court, and the 1563 and 1566 Parliaments for her to settle the matter by becoming a wife and mother, a duty expected of all Queens and of nearly all their female subjects. It was, however, the mixing up of this anxiety about the succession with anxiety lest the quarrel with Spain might escalate into war that proved the undoing of the anti-Cecil movement. This encouraged, if it did not actually produce, the idea of providing for the succession by letting Elizabeth stay as Virgin Queen for life, if that was what she wanted, but securing the future by marrying

15. J. L. Motley, *Rise of the Dutch Republic* (Everyman ed.), II.286.

the Duke of Norfolk, England's one remaining Duke, to Mary Stuart, who though an exile and semi-prisoner in England was still next heir-in-blood. A great many people, however, especially in the more populous and Protestant southern counties, were determined not to have the Roman Catholic Queen of Scots as Queen of England at any price. So the anti-Cecil movement lost much of its support, all the more as Cecil succeeded in driving a wedge between the Duke of Norfolk and the northern Catholics over their rival claims to the Dacre inheritance.

Some of the more extreme members of the movement did attempt to whip up renewed anger against Cecil by trying, through de Spes, to get Alba to intercept the Merchant Adventurers' summer fleet, bound now in 1569 under naval escort for Hamburg instead of for Antwerp. That, they reckoned, would bring down again upon the Secretary the fury of the merchants and the anger of the nobility. But Alba would not do as they asked; indeed, for lack of naval forces, he could not. So the Merchant Adventurers' move to Hamburg was not interrupted and, unlike their 1564 move to Emden, proved a very considerable success. England's foreign trade was demonstrably escaping from its Antwerp straitjacket and "another nail was driven into the coffin of the London-Antwerp trade."[16] Thereupon the motley anti-Cecil coalition melted away. Even its more reactionary elements fell apart, and when the northern Earls of Northumberland and Westmorland broke into open rebellion they found little support and showed little spirit—indeed, some believed that they only rebelled because they feared their fervently Catholic wives, who were near at hand, more than the Queen, who was far away.

The fiasco of the Revolt of the Northern Earls dealt a fatal blow to the reactionary Roman Catholic forces inside England. Their future efforts, from the Ridolfi plot of 1571–1572 onward, had to depend upon dwindling hopes of the assassination of the

16. C. Wilson, *Queen Elizabeth and the Revolt of the Netherlands*, p. 25.

Queen coupled with successful foreign invasion. The year 1569 also brought a decisive step out of that suffocating political and commercial dependence upon Spain and the Spanish Netherlands which had stifled English foreign policy and damped down English maritime enterprise for most of the past twenty years.

Off with the old also meant on with the new, meant exchanging the dying entente with Spain for an uneasy alliance with France (English alliances with France have usually had a tendency to be uneasy). The reversal of alliances came about in this manner. In September 1570 the third French War of Religion came to an end. During the next two years Louis of Nassau, the brother of William of Orange, and some of the Huguenot leaders—François de la Noue, du Plessis, and others: Coligny perhaps came in only toward the end and only reluctantly[17]—gained an increasing influence over the young and feeble King Charles IX. By the summer of 1572 they had brought him to the brink of allowing French intervention in the Netherlands to support a new invasion attempt by William. Louis offered, or at least suggested that, as the price of French help, France should get a good part of modern Belgium, including the coast of Flanders. In the hope of drawing Elizabeth in too, he also suggested that Holland and Zeeland might go to her in return for her assistance.

Elizabeth, however, had no desire to acquire Holland and Zeeland. She had even less desire to see the French acquire Flanders. But how was she to stop them? Being still in the midst of a quarrel with Spain, she could not think of taking on France as well—it took Charles I and Buckingham to do that. Indeed, Leicester and the new English resident ambassador in France, Francis Walsingham, would have had England join in heartily alongside France in a general anti-Habsburg alliance. But neither Elizabeth nor Cecil was willing to see French aggrandizement in the

17. N. M. Sutherland, *The Massacre of St. Bartholomew and the European Conflict, 1559–1572,* p. 147.

Netherlands, French power spreading eastward of Calais and the Straits of Dover. Nor did they trust the constancy of French policy—very sensibly, as the event turned out. So they adopted instead the policy of trying to check and control the French by cooperating with them in various more limited ways.

It is just possible that Elizabeth's expulsion of the Netherlands privateers, the Sea Beggars, from her southeastern ports in March 1572 and their seizure of Brielle on April 1 may have been a first step in this direction. Professor J. B. Black has argued strongly that this action was simply what it seemed to be, a movement of exasperation at the Sea Beggars' depredations and a friendly gesture to Alba and Spain.[18] Dr. Williamson, on the other hand, points out that no similar expulsion was decreed against the western privateers operating from Plymouth and west country ports. He argues that if Elizabeth had been truly anxious about the depredations and truly benevolent towards Spain, she would surely have denied all her ports to all Spain's enemies. Moreover, it was odd of her to send the order for the Sea Beggars to leave Dover by John Hawkins, whose last African–West Indies voyage had been treacherously destroyed by the Spaniards in the autumn of 1568 at San Juan de Ullua. In truth, however, the evidence is too slender to justify dogmatism either way. We can only say with Dr. Williamson that Elizabeth's expulsion of the Sea Beggars was an action "ostensibly beneficial to Spain, but in fact [one that] added enormously to Spain's difficulties."[19]

We are back on firmer ground, however, with the conclusion, also in April 1572, by the Treaty of Blois, of a defensive alliance with France. This, while silent about any offensive action, provided for mutual aid if either country were attacked by a third party. Elizabeth tried, though without much success, to broaden this into a wider defensive league, to include the German Prot-

18. J. B. Black, "Elizabeth, the Sea Beggars, and the Capture of Brielle," in *English Historical Review*, XLVI.30–47.

19. J. A. Williamson, *Hawkins*, pp. 261–267; *The Tudor Age*, p. 315.

estant princes, Denmark, Tuscany, and Venice. That would have prevented France from "going it alone." It was, in fact, the same policy that Castlereagh was to adopt two and a half centuries later toward Tsar Alexander I of Russia, the policy that he described as "grouping Alexander."[20]

At the same time, Elizabeth took steps to prevent the French from getting too much of a foothold in the coastal areas of the Netherlands that were vital to England's security. She pushed English "volunteers" under Sir Humphrey Gilbert into Flushing, more to deny that vital port to the French than to withhold it from the Spaniards. Through Henry Middlemore, she sent unofficial warning to Coligny that England could not tolerate French gains east of the Straits of Dover. She also began to make secret offers to Spain of support if the French did move into those sensitive areas—of support on condition that Spain restored the Netherlands to their former liberties and their former more or less unmilitarized state.

In the event, of course, the massacre of the Huguenots in Paris on St. Bartholomew's Day, 24 August 1572, ended for some years any further anxiety about French intervention in the Netherlands. Until the end of 1577 France was plunged back, with few lucid intervals, into renewed civil and religious strife. At the same time, Spain had its hands full with the continuing resistance in the Netherlands and with the aftermath of the Lepanto campaign of 1571 against the Turks in the Mediterranean. So Spain was ready enough to patch up an agreement with England in 1573.

These first fourteen years of Elizabeth's reign had thus done much to re-establish England's independence of both France and Spain. They laid the foundations of all that was to come after. They marked a long step toward the establishment of a united Great Britain, a Great Britain that was politically as well as geo-

20. "The Emperor has the greatest merit and must be held high; but he ought to be grouped and not made the sole feature for admiration"—Castlereagh to Liverpool, 20 April 1815, *Castlereagh Correspondence*, 3rd ser., I.478.

graphically an island. They saw the elimination, to a very large extent, of England's one land frontier and so the removal, to a very large extent, of the dangers of a stab in the back and of a war on two fronts. At the same time, Elizabeth had made use of the internal difficulties, political and religious, of both France and Spain in a way that had kept them both too preoccupied at home to risk adventures abroad. Yet she had done this without irritating either of them into open hostility. It is true that she had also been deprived—had, partly, deprived herself—of the availability of the Antwerp money market, for which no real substitute was available to her. That did in some measure impose limitations upon her freedom of action in foreign affairs. Nevertheless, she had shaken off dependence upon either Spain or France and had brought both to seek her friendship. So now there began a period of what today would be called détente and the next ten years or so were to be the high-water mark of Elizabeth's reign; both politically and economically they were the real "spacious days of great Elizabeth."

III.

The Coming of War

After 1572 it is, I think, true to say that Englishmen looked abroad with a new confidence. During the past fourteen years they had stood up to France and they had stood up to Spain. In the actual course of those confrontations they had, maybe, done no more, at best, than just about hold their own. Yet they *had* held their own and the outcome in each case had been that first France, then Spain came earnestly seeking friendlier relations even at some cost to their own interests.

It is true that in the more earnest of Protestant Englishmen this new-found confidence was tinged with those forebodings of eventual disaster that so often afflicted men who believed themselves to be the Lord's elect. They tended to be obsessed by the specter of a great international Papal-Spanish conspiracy, with its "fifth column" among the English Catholics. This was the driving force behind many of the volunteers who trooped across to fight under William the Silent in the Netherlands or alongside the Huguenots in France. It was the inspiration of the younger generation at home, of men such as Sir Philip Sidney who, according to his friend and biographer Fulke Greville, "never divided the consideration of state from the cause of religion."[1] It was the consideration uppermost in the minds of (rather less youthful) privy councillors such as Sir Francis Walsingham, who became Principal Secretary in 1573 and who spoke so often of "God's glory and

1. Fulke Greville, *Life of Sir Philip Sidney*, pp. 35–36.

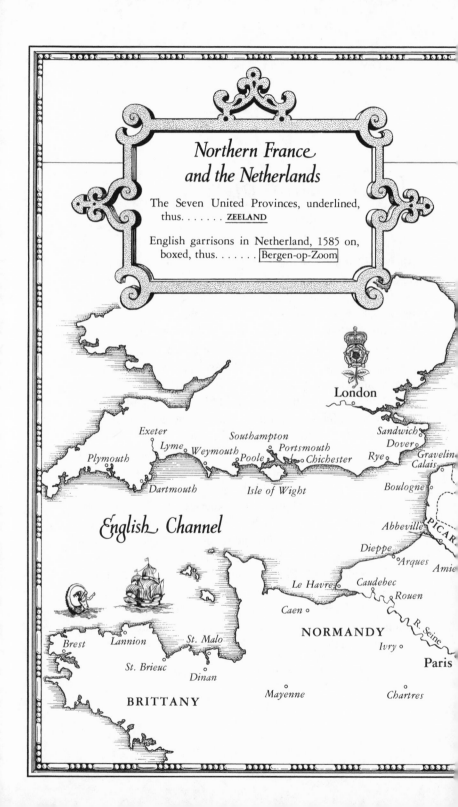

Northern France
and the Netherlands

The Seven United Provinces, underlined,
thus. . . . . . **ZEELAND**

English garrisons in Netherland, 1585 on,
boxed, thus. . . . . . Bergen-op-Zoom

London

Exeter Southampton Sandwich
Lyme Weymouth Portsmouth Dover
Plymouth Poole Chichester Rye Gravelin
Calais
Dartmouth Isle of Wight Boulogne

English Channel Abbeville PICAR

Dieppe
Arques Amie

Le Havre Caudebec
Caen Rouen
R. Seine
Brest Lannion St. Malo NORMANDY
St. Brieuc Ivry
Dinan Paris
BRITTANY Mayenne Chartres

next the Queen's safety,"[2] always in that order. For all these, England's true frontiers were on the Maas and the Loire, and the sooner and more vigorously the Roman Catholic menace was opposed there, the less likelihood there would be of having to fight it on English soil.

Elizabeth did not share, or at most only occasionally half shared, these fears and these sentiments. And for the better part of the next ten years after 1572 official Anglo-Spanish relations were considerably less tense than they had been during the previous decade. Bickerings at sea continued, but they were soft-pedalled by both governments. Elizabeth, for example, made some attempt to put down piracy, and she vetoed Sir Richard Grenville's project for a voyage into the Pacific which might well have followed a far from pacific course. Differences over religion were likewise not stressed. Indeed, Philip actually expelled the English Catholic exiles from their seminary at Douai in the Netherlands. Nor did he give much real encouragement to Irish rebels.

The one serious bone of contention was the Netherlands. Here Elizabeth's anxiety to get the Spanish army out, and her fears lest the rebels might let the French in, did gradually worsen her relations with Spain. For most of the 1570s, however, even this was not an unduly urgent matter. From 1572 until 1576 the Spanish army had its hands full with the desperate resistance led by William of Orange in Holland and Zeeland. Then in the summer and autumn of 1576, after the sudden death of Alba's successor Don Luis de Requesens, that army's mutiny and its sacking of Antwerp in the "Spanish Fury" provoked a general Netherlands revolt. The Pacification of Ghent in November brought an alliance of the newly revolted provinces with Holland and Zeeland and so the creation of a semi-independent United Netherlands. This United Netherlands compelled the Spanish army to withdraw from their territories. It was just what Elizabeth wanted, just

2. Quoted in Conyers Read, *Mr. Secretary Walsingham*, I.133.

what she had been working for during the past nine or ten years.

A year later, in July 1577, the new Spanish governor-general, Requesens's successor Don John of Austria, did recall the army and in 1579 the United Netherlands split into the rival Unions of Arras and Utrecht. Even so, it was not until 1581 that the Union of Arras invited Don John's successor, Alexander Farnese, Duke of Parma, to bring the army back from the remote southeastern province of Luxembourg and to approach the heart of the Netherlands and the seacoast of Flanders. Until then that army hardly presented any immediate threat to its neighbors, least of all to England. Don John, it is true, had dreamed of conquering England, marrying Mary Stuart, and usurping Elizabeth's crown. But circumstances in the Netherlands and the unwillingness of Philip II to assent to his schemes meant that these were never more than dreams.

The unity of the United Netherlands, however, was always very precarious. Precariousness was indeed built into the very nature and origins of their revolt. Or, rather, their revolts: for essentially the Revolt of the Netherlands was a bundle of local reactions against the policies of a centralizing and alien government. There was a fundamental particularism, a parish-pump outlook, in the attitudes of the various provinces. On top of this basic particularism there was the fact that the United Netherlands which came into existence in 1576 rested upon an uneasy coalition of the Calvinist-dominated burgher oligarchies of Holland and Zeeland with the conservative Catholic nobility and urban patriciates of the other provinces. As an ally, the United Netherlands were as brittle and as unreliable as French Huguenots or Protestant Scots.

So Elizabeth's policy throughout the 1570s and early 1580s, despite the pressure from Leicester and Walsingham for active, armed intervention, was primarily directed at getting Spain to agree to an early withdrawal of its military forces and a return to the largely home-ruling Netherlands of Charles V's time. She

tried repeatedly to bring Philip to recognize the difficulty of sub-
jugating the Netherlands and the danger that the attempt might
let in the French. This was very clearly presented to him as early
as the summer of 1575 by a special ambassador, Sir Henry Cobham. Cobham's instructions were

> to show the King that, however he has been informed of
> [Elizabeth's] doings with his subjects in the Low Countries,
> if he knew how often and earnestly she had been solicited to
> take possession of Holland and Zeeland, he might say he
> never had such a friend as she had been. If some speedy
> remedy be not taken, those Countries will be at the devotion
> of the French King who, and his predecessor, have contin-
> ually aided the Prince of Orange with money to maintain
> his wars and now continues the same with a monthly secret
> pay. As nothing can be so hurtful to the King and dangerous
> to herself as this, she earnestly desires him to divert this
> course now in hand by allowing his subjects to enjoy their
> ancient privileges and suffering them to live freely from the
> extremities of the Inquisition. In this behalf he is to say that
> she will be content to use any office of mediation for com-
> pounding these differences.[3]

At the same time, despite the advocacy of Walsingham and his
friends, Elizabeth had little sympathy for William of Orange and
his Calvinist supporters, particularly when their blockading ships
interfered with England's reopened Antwerp trade, even though
Hamburg was now the main center of the Merchant Adventurers'
traffic. She did take a somewhat more sympathetic attitude after
the general Netherlands uprising in the autumn of 1576 and the
conclusion of the Pacification of Ghent. She lent some money to
the insurgent States General at Brussels and she promised more.
She even on occasion promised troops, especially to counter any

3. *Calendar of State Papers, Foreign Series*, XI.76–77.

move by the Guises and the French Catholics to intervene on the side of Don John. In the main, however, she still relied upon efforts, upon redoubled efforts to mediate a settlement.

Professor Wilson considers this policy to have been a mistake. He argues that vigorous armed intervention by England in 1577–1578 would have rallied the Netherlands around William of Orange and so created a truly United Netherlands.[4] This is a view that seems to me to underestimate very seriously the depth of the divisions, religious, social, and political, within the United Netherlands and the strength of the particularist motivation of the movement. It seems to me also to overestimate no less seriously William of Orange's control over his radical Calvinist adherents outside Holland and Zeeland, more especially in Flanders, where they were a particularly active and vociferous minority. It also, of course, ignores Elizabeth's desire to retain nominal Spanish sovereignty over the Netherlands to ensure their better defense against possible French aggression—but that, in Professor Wilson's opinion, was not a worthy object of English policy either.

A further, no less serious, point is that active armed English intervention in Netherlands affairs at this time would certainly have brought on, if not an actual shooting war with Spain, at least another trade embargo just at the moment when Hamburg, under renewed pressure from the other Hanseatic Towns, was refusing to renew its ten years' agreement with the Merchant Adventurers. It was a moment when a return to Antwerp, devastated by the Spanish Fury, offered no more than a very limited alternative and when Emden was no more adequate than it had proved in 1564. Moreover, England's search for alternative "vents" and alternative sources of imports outside the Netherlands and northwest Germany was only just beginning. Between 1553 and 1576 interest in new overseas ventures had been sporadic,

4. C. Wilson, *Queen Elizabeth and the Revolt of the Netherlands*, chapters 3 and 4.

and it was only in the later 1570s that a new and more vigorous era began. The Spanish Company was not established until 1577, nor the Eastland Company (for trade into the Baltic and to Danzig) till 1579. The first overtures for trade to the Levant were not made till 1578; the Turkey Company was not formed until 1581 nor the Venice Company until 1583. Martin Frobisher's three voyages in search of the northwest passage around America to the Orient occurred only in 1576–1578, while Sir Humphrey Gilbert's North American and Newfoundland projects dated from the same period. So the imposition of embargos on Spanish trade would have been a serious matter at this stage of England's commercial and maritime development.

Anyway, the argument in favor of such a preventive intervention assumes, as Walsingham and his friends assumed, that there was something to prevent. Now, it is true that ten years later Philip II did send his Armada against England. But that was by no means inevitable in 1577–1578. It was not then even possible, for at that time he had no Armada. All that he had in the way of oceangoing ships of war—apart from the well-nigh useless Mediterranean galleys—was a half-dozen or so galleons of the Indian Guard, earmarked for escorting the American convoys and silver shipments.

In the latter part of 1577 and early in 1578 matters did become a little more urgent. At the end of July 1577 Don John broke his accord with the Brussels States General, seized Namur, and recalled the Spanish troops to the Netherlands. In September, the fifth French War of Religion came to an end, and although Henry III was not tempted to risk a confrontation with Spain by adventuring in the Low Countries, his younger brother and heir-presumptive, Francis of Anjou, was clearly open to offers now that French domestic waters were no longer sufficiently troubled for his fishing.

Elizabeth's first reaction to this revival of French interest was to despatch Thomas Wilkes to impress yet again on Philip the danger of French intervention if he did not immediately come to a reasonable settlement in the Netherlands. Wilkes went off in December 1577 and achieved nothing. Also, however, in December the Queen unleashed Francis Drake for what was to turn out to be his voyage round the world. Was this intended as a rather less gentle hint than Wilkes was delivering? Certainly the promoters of Drake's voyage were "all associated with maritime enterprise of a predatory kind and all, with the exception of the Queen, advocated a vigorously anti-Spanish policy."[5] And whatever Drake's purposes may have been, it is unlikely that they were totally innocent of any idea of troubling the Spaniards in the New World. Yet it was only a couple of years or so since Elizabeth had vetoed an apparently somewhat similar project of Sir Richard Grenville.

In January 1578, however, Don John routed the States' army at Gembloux. Seven months later this victory was to be somewhat counterbalanced by a defeat his forces suffered at Rijmenant in August 1578. But in the interval between the two battles the United Netherlands showed rapidly increasing signs of breaking apart. The need for speedy and more direct, more positive, help seemed to grow much more urgent. Elizabeth was still not willing to commit herself to open intervention by sending in English troops. But she did secretly subsidise the bringing in of a German mercenary army under that "stipendiary warrior," the Calvinist John Casimir of the Palatinate. The outcome was not a happy one. Casimir's troops, ill paid by the Brussels States General, soon attached themselves to the radical Calvinist minority in Flanders. They therefore soon became as unwelcome to the predominantly Catholic southern provinces as Don John's Spanish

5. K. R. Andrews, "The Aims of Drake's Expedition of 1577–80," in *American Historical Review*, LXXIII.739.

army. The result of John Casimir's intervention was to hasten the Brussels States General in August 1578 into an agreement with Francis of Anjou.

So the French were in after all. And Elizabeth was faced with much the same problem as in 1571–1572: how to ensure that, as Sussex put it, neither "the French possess or the Spaniards tyrannise in the Low Countries"?[6] The way she now attempted to solve it was very peculiarly her own. Indeed, her solution appalled most of her councillors, except for Sussex and possibly Burghley. She found that the Brussels States General had called in Anjou only as "Defender of Belgic Liberties," that is, only as an ally and protector, not as their sovereign. Also he was dropping broad hints that he would not be averse to marrying her. So might she not, by seeming to rise to that bait, both control him and use him to put extra pressure upon Spain to come to a reasonable settlement with the Netherlands insurgents? After all, it was tolerably obvious that Anjou's advances resulted from his disappointments at his brother's hands; and that Henry III was never prepared to risk a war with Spain by giving him very substantial backing, let alone open backing, not even when in January 1581 the States General offered and Anjou accepted the titular sovereignty over their country. Anjou's Netherlands adventure was clearly a private venture of his own, not a part of French national policy, though he was heir-presumptive to the throne of France.

How seriously Elizabeth regarded this Anjou courtship is hard to determine. For a good part of the time, there is not much doubt, she found it great fun. Possibly, too, now that she was in her mid-forties she was less choosy than in her younger days. Yet it is hard to believe that she did not, in the final analysis, feel that marriage to this unprepossessing, undersized, pockmarked little Valois prince would be too high a price to pay for the very limited advantages it could bring. Chiefly, no doubt, she regarded the

6. *Calendar of State Papers, Foreign Series,* XIII.120.

courtship as an instrument in her Netherlands policy, as a means of limiting and controlling French action there and at the same time stepping up the pressure upon Philip of Spain.

In those respects it was financially expensive and its success was decidedly limited. The indirect Anglo-French intervention exasperated Philip II. It also aggravated the divisions in the United Netherlands. It moved the Union of Arras—the union of the Walloon provinces of Artois and Hainault—in 1581 to call up Parma and his army. From the improved base that gave him to move down across the flat lands of Belgium, he had by 1585 reconquered so much of the Netherlands, including Brussels and Antwerp, that resistance was confined to not much more than the beleaguered Holland and Zeeland and Utrecht that had faced Alba after the St. Bartholomew's Day Massacre. By then, too, in France Anjou's premature—or at any rate early—death in May 1584 brought results not wholly dissimilar to the results of that massacre. For it left the Huguenot chieftain, Henry of Navarre, as heir-presumptive to the throne of the childless Henry III. That was a prospect that most of the great Roman Catholic majority of Frenchmen found it hard to stomach. It was a prospect that the French Catholic League, headed by the Guise family, found utterly intolerable; and so it plunged France back into another, longer, and even bloodier War of Religion.

There, however, the similarity between 1585 and 1572 ends. The outcome of the 1572 crisis, so far as Anglo-Spanish relations were concerned, had been peace; the outcome of the 1585 crisis was war. For this there were two main reasons. One was that the Catholic League by the Treaty of Joinville in December 1584 accepted Philip II of Spain as its protector and paymaster. Never before had Philip had quite this hold over a French faction; never before had he had quite such an assurance that he need fear no French interference if he turned to settle his long account with England. Indeed, as the main strength of the League was in northern and northeastern France, he might well hope to have the French Channel coast and the French Channel ports at his disposal.

The second reason was that Philip had at last acquired the means of attacking England directly. In 1578 the young King Sebastian of Portugal had been killed on a campaign against the Moors in North Africa. His successor, the old Cardinal Henry, died two years later, like him childless. Thereupon Philip II of Spain had sent in his armies, under the Duke of Alba, to assert his genealogical claim to the Portuguese throne. Alba easily overcame the resistance of the Portuguese pretender, the illegitimate Don Antonio, and before the summer of 1580 was over King Philip of Spain found himself King also of Portugal. With the Portuguese crown he acquired the Portuguese royal navy of twelve oceangoing galleons. By adding these to the Indian Guard, now ten or a dozen galleons strong, he at a stroke doubled his Atlantic naval fighting forces and brought the number of his royal warships to within measurable distance of the number of the English Queen's navy royal. He now had the nucleus of an oceangoing armada of sailing war galleons capable of operating in Atlantic waters and over Atlantic distances, where the oared galleys of his Mediterranean navy were of little use. New building and purchases during the next few years augmented this into an Armada sizable enough to make the "Enterprise of England" conceivable.

So, by the middle 1580s Philip had both the opportunity and the means of trying to put a stop to England's persistent interference in his Netherlands affairs and to English sailors' depredations at sea and against his American possessions. Moreover, by the middle 1580s he was coming round to Granvelle's view that the root of his Netherlands troubles lay in England. The final provocation came in the summer and autumn of 1585, when by the Treaty of Nonsuch Elizabeth took the Dutch into her protection and sent the Earl of Leicester with 7,000 English troops to stiffen their resistance to Parma. To send an army officially into another ruler's dominions to assist rebels against that ruler was an act of hostility that no sovereign could well ignore. So, although Elizabeth perhaps intended the despatch of Leicester and his troops as merely a stepping up of the pressure on Spain to agree to a reasonable settlement, in fact that action meant war.

War meant new circumstances, new conditions that weakened the Queen's personal control over the formulation and execution of foreign policy, and of strategy which with her was very much a continuation of foreign policy. This was particularly true of English strategy in the years which followed the victory over Spain's "Invincible" Armada in 1588 and of the occasions then when the initiative lay in her hands. It was so partly—though only partly—because she was a woman and war was preeminently a masculine preserve. It was not that she lacked judgment in military matters. At least she could pick out the essentials clearly enough—the need to destroy the remains of the 1588 Armada in 1589 or to defeat Parma's army in 1591. But she had not quite the same confidence in matters of strategy as she had in matters of foreign policy. In part, also, this was due to the slowness of sixteenth-century communications and the delays and irregularities in the flow of intelligences about her enemy's actions and intentions, and, no less, those of her allies and her own commanders. Communications within England, a comparatively small country, were reasonably speedy and reliable. Communications with the Continent, on the other hand, were very much at the mercy of winds and waves. Strong westerlies could stop news from Holland and Zeeland for two or three weeks at a time, as they did when the town of Geertruidenberg was lost in March 1589. Leaguer troops and predatory peasants, too, created many perils for couriers journeying overland to the French Channel ports from Chartres or Noyon or Sedan or wherever the very peripatetic King Henry IV of France happened to be. All this often deprived the Queen of that firm basis of information which she needed for decisive judgments. It goes far toward explaining her frequent hesitations and changes of mind. She felt constrained to suggest rather than to command. As Professor MacCaffrey says, "Once the focus of action moved to the distant frontiers of Scotland, or worse still beyond the seas, she was seized with doubts, anxieties, and hesitations. Necessarily, such actions could be carried out only by men; the limitations of her femininity came unpleasantly home to her at these times."[7] A queen, a woman, could hardly command an army in the field, let alone a fleet at sea. No English queen had commanded an army in the field since the days of Boadicea, and even kings did not command fleets at sea. Elizabeth had therefore to rely upon lieutenants, upon generals and admirals over whom her control diminished in direct proportion to their distance from her court. The disobedience to her instructions by Leicester in the Netherlands in 1586 and by Sir John Norris and Sir Francis Drake in Portugal in 1589 are among the more spectacular instances of this difficulty of control. A century later another Queen of England solved the problem by finding a Marlborough, but Elizabeth I was no Anne and Elizabethan England produced no Marlborough.

A much more serious limitation was finance. Ordinary peacetime foreign policy and diplomacy cost something, but not much. After the 1560s Elizabeth kept resident ambassadors only in France, and from 1585 in the United Provinces (there was also a resident from 1583 at Constantinople, but he was paid by the Turkey Company, or from 1592 by the then newly amalgamated Levant Company). Special embassies usually did not last very long, and often cost the ambassador more than the Crown. When they did last a long time, as did Dr. Christopher Parkins's mission to Denmark, the Hanse Towns, and Poland in 1591–1592, they were usually run on economical lines. There were, of course, also couriers and posts to be paid and these could sometimes be

7. W. MacCaffrey, *The Shaping of the Elizabethan Regime*, p. 299.

costly enough to draw suggestions from the Secretary that the ambassador or agent should write rather less often. But by and large they were not a major item of government expenditure. Nor, until the later 1580s were intelligencers and spies; until then they hardly formed a system or a network. So the expense of ordinary peacetime diplomacy was not at all exorbitant.

War, on the other hand, was *very* expensive. Troops, ships, supplies, subsidies all cost vast sums of money and Burghley reckoned that all these had trebled in price since the middle of the century. The aid promised to the Dutch by the 1585 Treaty of Nonsuch was forecast to cost £126,000 a year, and it cost appreciably more in Leicester's time. The Armada campaign cost the Exchequer £161,000, besides what fell upon the local rates and ship money. The total Exchequer issues rose from a mere £149,000—I am using Professor Dietz's figures[8]—in 1583 to £420,000 in 1588 and to £570,688.17s.7d. in 1599 with the rebellion of Tyrone in Ireland—and by then the Exchequer was empty and the government debt £177,000.[9]

These sums, of course, seem ridiculously small by twentieth-century standards. To appreciate their significance we need to set them against the Queen's income during those years of the Spanish war. When the war began, her "ordinary" revenues (that is, her income from Crown lands, feudal incidents, customs duties, the profits of justice, but not including parliamentary taxes) were only about £200,000 or at most £250,000 a year. Most of this was needed for the ordinary running expenses of the central government, the central judiciary, the court, the normal upkeep of the navy and the ordnance office, and small garrisons at Berwick-on-Tweed and in Ireland.

How, then, was the gap between this "ordinary" revenue and the extraordinary expenditures of wartime bridged? The Queen

8. F. C. Dietz, *The Exchequer under Elizabeth*, pp. 100, 101, 103.
9. R. B. Outhwaite, "The Price of Crown Land at the Turn of the 16th Century," in *Economic History Review* (n.s.), XX.239.

began the war with almost £300,000 of "chested treasure" in the Exchequer, the savings of ten years or so of economical government augmented by a substantial slice of Drake's spoils from his 1577–1580 voyage. All this had gone by 1590. Then the Queen sold Crown lands: over £645,000 worth of them in 1590–1591 and 1599–1601.[10] That, of course, was undesirable, a living on capital which could hardly be replaced, for the abbey lands had been confiscated long ago by Henry VIII. Nor was it possible to borrow abroad as Henry VIII, Edward VI, and Mary had done so lavishly. Elizabeth did try in 1589 to borrow £100,000 in Germany, but the attempt was a failure. So Elizabeth had to rely increasingly upon her subjects to finance the war. This meant a steep increase in parliamentary taxation and an even steeper increase in other ways of raising money from them, for example, by the sale of monopolies. It meant also a steep increase in the government's demands for the more or less unpaid services of local officials and gentry, as well as for more local rates to equip, clothe, and arm troop levies. We will come back to these matters and their repercussions later on.

Let us turn now to look more specifically at the war at sea. Here the Queen had to rely upon her subjects in an even more direct way. For she had not enough ships of her own and could not have afforded the extra pay of their crews or the extra cost of their victualling and equipping if she had possessed them. She therefore had to leave the war at sea very largely to private enterprise, herself joining in as a partner in some of the larger and more strategically purposeful operations. In the first two or three years after the defeat of the 1588 Armada she did send out squadrons of her ships to lie off the Spanish coast and around the Azores. In 1589, after the return of the big expedition under Norris and Drake to Portugal, Frobisher was out with two of the Queen's ships and a pinnace. Again, in 1590, after a pause for a

10. W. R. Scott, *English, Scottish, and Irish Joint Stock Companies to 1720,* I.96.

false alarm about Spanish preparations for a new Armada, Hawkins took six royal galleons to the Spanish coast to keep an eye on the fleet in Ferrol, while Frobisher went to the Azores with another six in a fruitless attempt to intercept the homeward-bound flotas from America. In 1591 again, Lord Thomas Howard and Sir Richard Grenville were at the Azores with five of the Queen's ships. By then, however, Spain had made good the 1588 losses and had a fleet in being again, a fleet too numerous and too strong for a mere squadron of English vessels. The English were driven off their station and—in one of the most famous of sea fights, celebrated by Sir Walter Raleigh in prose and centuries later by Lord Tennyson in verse—the Queen's *Revenge* was lost and Grenville died of his wounds on the deck of the Spanish flagship.

All these, however, were primarily commerce-destroying operations, a sort of royal privateering. The war at sea, in fact, was mainly a privateering, commerce-destroying war. The Queen's subjects proved adept at it. The English, a German visitor wrote in 1598, "are good sailors and better pirates, cunning, treacherous, and thievish."[11] Their operations, moreover, were on a considerable scale. Dr. K. R. Andrews in his book on *Elizabethan Privateering* estimates that they made at least one hundred privateering voyages a year in the 1590s, apart from the operations of the royal navy.[12] The number may, indeed, have risen in some years as high as two hundred. Most of the ships involved were converted or, more simply, armed merchant vessels. And in the earlier years especially, only a small proportion of them were of any real size. Out of 139 that were operating in the three years from 1589 to 1591 and whose tonnages are known, only 41 were over 100 tons, only 16 over 200 tons. The proportion of large ships increased in later years, but there were still very few of over

11. Paul Hentzner in 1598, in W. B. Rye, *England as Seen by Foreigners*, p. 110.
12. K. R. Andrews, *Elizabethan Privateering*, pp. 32–34.

The North Atlantic

1500   500   500   1500
1000   0   1000

North
Atlantic Ocean

Newfoundland

London
Hamburg
Scilly Is.   Antwerp
Brest   Gravelines
Bay of Biscay   Calais
La Rochelle
Santander   Bayonne
Azores   Ferrol   Leghorn
Flores   Coruña   Sebastian
Terceira   Lisbon   Cadiz
St. Michael
Virginia   Madeira   Gibralter
Bermuda   Tenerife
Canary
Florida   Islands

Havana   Bahamas
Hispaniola
Panama   Porto Rico
Nombre de Dios   C. Verde Is.
Cartagena

N

W   E

S

300 tons. There were, that is to say, very few of them that could stand up to even a medium-sized war galleon, very few that could compare even with the Queen's small galleon, the *Foresight*, let alone with the great Spanish *San Felipe* and the others that the *Revenge* fought so long and so gallantly. As a result, this privateering was a commerce-destroying affair and not an attack upon the Spanish war navy.

As a commerce-destroying operation it was reasonably successful. By the end of the war Spain's merchant navy—apart from the convoyed and protected American fleet—was virtually destroyed, and Spain's overseas trade, at least its trade to continental Europe, was increasingly in foreign hands.[13] But Spain's war navy was as strong as ever, if not stronger. The "Invincible" Armada of 1588 was the first but by no means the last of Spain's armadas, though none of the later ones looked as threatening or came as near. The 1596 Armada, sent to avenge the English sacking of Cadiz earlier in the year, was dispersed by autumnal storms before it got into the Channel. So, too, was that of 1597, after it had sailed across the Bay of Biscay side by side with the English fleet under Essex returning from the Islands Voyage without either side sighting the other. In 1601 yet another Armada escorted Spanish troops to Ireland, and in 1602 Leveson met it again off the Azores and found it too strong to allow him to attack the homeward-bound American fleet which it was escorting.

This privateering character of the war at sea also, of course, made a coordinated, government-directed strategy very difficult, if not impossible. The privateers did not favor too much concentration of force, because it meant that there would be too many to share the spoils. The quarrels in 1592 over the cargo of the rich Portuguese East Indian carrack, the *Madre de Dios*, emphasized this. Certainly the privateers did swarm like wasps round

---

13. Ibid., pp. 223–226.

particular honey pots: off Cadiz and Cape St. Vincent; around the Azores; off Havana and in the Florida Channel. Profit, however, rather than victory, was their main purpose. A few, mostly courtiers or officials, did sometimes rise to something like strategical ideas. The Virginia projects of Sir Richard Grenville and Sir Walter Raleigh, though by no means unconnected with thoughts of plunder, had a somewhat loftier purpose. So had the Howards' operations in 1591 and 1596, and some of the Earl of Cumberland's expeditions. But these were the exceptions and more and more, as the years passed, it was the merchants who took over and dominated, with profit as their predominant motive. The Queen could not pay the piper—she could not even afford all the pipes—so she could not call the tune.

This was true even in the more strategically purposeful operations in which she was a leading partner, in, for example, the Portugal expedition of 1589. Let us look at the genesis of this expedition in a little more detail.[14] We shall, I think, find it rather more complex than Sir Julian Corbett's vision of it as a simple, single-minded masterstroke planned by Sir Francis Drake.[15] It originated, as Walsingham put it to Lord Admiral Howard, in "the desire Her Majesty had for the intercepting of the King [of Spain]'s treasure from the Indies" after the defeat of the 1588 Armada.[16] Its origin thus lay in the Queen's wish to seize the ships bringing the annual tribute of silver from the American mines to Spain, what Fulke Greville called the method "of Jason, by fetching away his golden fleece."[17] It was an idea that John Hawkins and others had been peddling for twenty years and, as the treasure on those ships might amount to perhaps as much as £3,000,000

14. I have discussed this expedition at greater length in "Queen Elizabeth and the Portugal Expedition of 1589," in *English Historical Review*, LXVI.1–26, 194–218.

15. Sir J. Corbett, *Drake and the Tudor Navy*, II.294–296.

16. *State Papers relating to the Defeat of the Spanish Armada*, II.167.

17. Fulke Greville, *Life of Sir Philip Sidney*, p. 90.

sterling in Elizabethan money, it was a tempting enough prize for a Queen whose resources were already severely stretched.

At the end of August 1588, while the Armada was still struggling along the Atlantic coasts of Scotland and Ireland, privy councillors, sailors, and soldiers—it is not possible to name them exactly—met to discuss the Queen's idea. At once it became clear that after the Armada campaign there were no ships, royal or privately owned, that could reasonably face an Atlantic voyage without an overhaul. All needed thorough cleansing inside and out, if not a full refit, for all had been at sea since March and some since Christmas. This meant that they could not be in any strength at the Azores, the Atlantic staging post of the American fleets, until well into October. That would be late anyway. Englishmen and Spaniards both regarded the months from November to February as a closed season for operations in the open Atlantic, and 1588 was a particularly rough and stormy year. Besides, the silver ships came but once a year and were usually home well before October. They had, or tried, to get through the Florida Channel and out past Bermuda before the hurricane season.

Yet England could not well put off its counterstroke to the 1588 Armada until July or August 1589. There were obvious reasons of prestige that ruled out such a delay. Moreover, by July or August the campaigning season in the Netherlands and northern France would be well under way and there might well be major crises there if they were not forestalled by earlier and effective English action against the mainland of Spain or against Spain's ocean communications with the New World. Most important of all, by July or August 1589 the Spaniards could have refitted, repaired, and reinforced whatever part of the 1588 Armada had reached home. Spain, in other words, by then could have a fleet in being again, a fleet strong enough at least to escort home the treasure ships and the American convoys. Clearly, therefore, if the English wanted to make reasonably sure of seizing those trea-

sure ships and those American convoys, they ought first to complete the work of 1588 by destroying the remainder of the 1588
Armada, the part that had got back to Spain.

As early as 9 August 1588 Burghley had wanted to send ships
to catch the shot-torn and weatherbeaten remnants of the Armada
as they struggled home between Ireland and Spain.[18] No one,
however, had shown any enthusiasm for the idea. It would not
have been easy to find ships fit enough to face the weather in the
Western Approaches and the Bay of Biscay. Everyone, too, was
probably weary from the long exertions of spring and summer. At
all events, nothing was done. But if an expedition could be got
off by, say, February, that would be time enough; for the Spanish
fleet could hardly be made seaworthy, let alone battleworthy, by
then. All the same, by then it would presumably be in well-de-
fended ports and in early September 1588 the most probable port
appeared to be Lisbon. Now, as the 1587 operations off the Spanish coast, "the singeing of the King of Spain's beard," had shown,
even Drake did not regard forcing a way up the winding, narrow-
ing, fortified Tagus to Lisbon as a job for ships alone. It called for
land forces to ease the ships' way past the forts and batteries. So,
to destroy the remains of the 1588 Armada in order to make more
practicable the capture of the 1589 American convoys would now
require land forces, quite considerable land forces, an army in
fact.

An army, however, would require transports, that is more ships
as well as more money than the Queen could scrape together
after all the expenses of the Armada year. Hence the expedition
became a sort of joint-stock partnership, with the Queen providing one-third of the £60,000 it was estimated to cost—in the
event it cost nearly £100,000 and her contribution was nearer
£60,000—and Sir John Norris and Sir Francis Drake and their
friends and backers putting up the rest. This, of course, weakened

18. *State Papers relating to the Defeat of the Spanish Armada*, II.85.

the Queen's control over the expedition. Besides, if it was to include an army, why should that army not be something more than a mere landing-party to shepherd the fleet past the Tagus forts? Why should it not be used to try to restore the Portuguese pretender Don Antonio to the Portuguese throne, from which the Spaniards had evicted him in 1580?

It is true that bringing in Don Antonio could help to bring in the money needed to finance the expedition. Not that Don Antonio had any money. But the prospect of establishing under his aegis privateering and trading bases in Portugal or the Azores or Brazil, that could well open the purses of those London and southern England merchants who had lost their Spanish trade because of the war, many of whom had turned already to privateering or to promoting privateering. Gentlemen and yeomen, too, would be attracted by the prospects for plundering the Spaniard. Yet here was still another objective for the expedition: the conquest of Portugal. It was, moreover, an objective that became more and more predominant as volunteers flocked to join Norris and Drake until they had twice as many troops as they had bargained for or catered for. In the end they had something like 19,000 men, in addition to their ships' crews. Such an army required a large number of transports. It swelled the fleet to unwieldy numbers, comparable in fact to Spain's 1588 Armada, though with fewer fighting ships.

Possibly, too, the inclusion of Don Antonio introduced an even more far-reaching dream. For in an agreement made by him with Norris and Drake a few months later, he agreed that if they could not win Portugal itself for him, they were to take him and the army to some other part of his dominions; if he then desired to stay there and the generals wished to go further and reduce his other dominions and isles of the East Indies, they were to leave him 4,000 men and 10 ships.[19] Here, then, there was

19. *Calendar of State Papers, Foreign Series*, XXIII.140.

envisaged the possibility of another attempt to follow up Drake's understanding, arrived at during his voyage round the world, with the Sultan of Ternate and to open up direct trade to the East Indies. One attempt had been made already, by Edward Fenton in 1582. But that had ended in disaster and had never got out of the Atlantic. It looks, however, as if Drake himself had not abandoned the idea.

So, because the Queen's ships could not be ready to set out upon an Atlantic voyage in September 1588 and because she could not afford the larger and more costly expedition needed in the spring of 1589, Elizabeth's simple straightforward "desire . . . for the intercepting of the King of Spain's treasure from the Indies" had grown into a complex and multipurpose enterprise. For the Queen and for Burghley, its main job was to destroy Spain's war navy in its harbors and then to go on to intercept the silver ships from America at the Azores. Drake shared the Azores aim, but also looked farther afield, looked as far as the East Indies. And for Norris, the young Earl of Essex, and the soldiers the great aim was to conquer Portugal.

This interpretation of the genesis and purposes of the expedition differs considerably, as I said, from that of Sir Julian Corbett and most of the other naval historians. They regarded the whole conception as Drake's and considered that Drake's primary and overriding aim was Portugal. It is a view for which there seems to me to be little really solid evidence. It also makes it very difficult to understand Drake's hesitation and delay in risking his ships in the Tagus, even when he knew that the army was before Lisbon. One of the naval historians here falls back upon a theory of increasing age and failing powers—Drake, poor old chap, was forty-eight!—illustrating it by Drake's misdating a letter as June 1587 instead of the less fortunate June 1589.[20] Surely a more convinc-

---

20. M. Oppenheim, in *The Naval Tracts of Sir William Monson* (Navy Records Society), I. 221–222.

ing explanation is that he wanted to keep his ships intact for intercepting the American convoys at the Azores. And surely the expedition's multiplicity of purposes gives it all the hallmarks of a committee product. It has been suggested that a camel might be a horse designed by a committee: the Portugal expedition of 1589 was very like a camel.

This Portugal expedition not only illustrates how the Queen's inability to equip and finance such an enterprise from her own resources meant giving it a multiplicity of purposes that would make it all things to all the partners in it. It also illustrates, not less vividly, the serious limitations in the Queen's control over the execution of policy in wartime. The commanders of the 1589 expedition blatantly disregarded her instructions, instructions insistently reiterated both orally and in writing, that the destruction of the remnants of the 1588 Armada must be their first and principal task. It was certainly unfortunate that those remnants had not been able to make their way to Lisbon. Battered and storm-strained, they had been driven to leeward into the corner of the Bay of Biscay, to Santander and San Sebastian. It was admittedly difficult for Drake to take his greatly swollen fleet into that corner. But he never even made the attempt; he never got nearer to it than Coruña (the Groyne, to sixteenth-century Englishmen), where there was almost nothing to destroy and where the expedition aimlessly wasted its first two valuable weeks. It then made a hash of attacking Lisbon; never looked like restoring Don Antonio to the throne of Portugal; and never got to the Azores, let alone the East Indies.

So the half of the 1588 Armada that had managed to struggle home was left to refit quietly in the Biscay ports. As an English agent, Edmund Palmer, wrote from St. Jean-de-Luz, "If Sir Francis had gone to Santander as he went to the Groyne, he had done such a service as never subject had done. For with twelve sail of his ships, he might have destroyed all the forces which the Spaniards had there, which was the whole strength of the country by sea. There they did ride all unrigged and their ordnance on the shore and some twenty men in a ship only to keep them. It was far overseen that he had not gone thither first."[21]

Indeed it was. By the autumn of 1589 those helpless Spanish ships had been sufficiently refitted to be able to struggle round to Ferrol. By 1591, reinforced by newly built galleons and by ships purchased, they were strong enough to force Lord Thomas Howard's squadron off the Azores station and to capture the Queen's *Revenge*. Spain by then had a fleet in being again and the "method of Jason" would now require greater forces than Elizabeth could provide.

Moreover, with the revival of Spain's oceanic naval power the question of the security of the French Channel coast acquired a new urgency just at the time when the affairs of France were coming to a crisis. That, however, is a subject for the next chapter.

21. *Calendar of State Papers, Foreign Series*, XXIII.383.

IV.

Ocean and Continent

It may seem odd that it was in France rather than in the Netherlands that English intervention in the war on land in western Europe reached its peak during the years 1591 and 1592. After all, the Netherlands, or the presence of the Spanish army in the Netherlands, had ever since the late 1560s been the principal bone of contention between England and Spain; and it was chiefly because Elizabeth sent an army under the Earl of Leicester to the Netherlands in 1585 that Philip II sent an Armada under the Duke of Medina Sidonia against England in 1588.

Let us note that date 1585. For it was not upon the near-collapse of the Netherlands resistance to Spain after the assassination of William the Silent in 1584 that Elizabeth sent her army to help the Dutch. It was upon the collapse of the French monarchy with the outbreak of the War of the League in 1585. It is true that in sending those troops she was doing what Walsingham and Leicester had long been urging. Yet it is no less true that in not sending them until 1585 she was following the counsel of Burghley. For at the time of the Privy Council debates of October 1584 and mid-March 1585 Burghley had been doubtful about both the necessity and the wisdom of armed and open intervention in Netherlands affairs. He had then been inclined to leave the Dutch to their fate if France would not or could not join in helping them. He had then been inclined to trust that Philip, despite his many grounds for complaint against Elizabeth and her subjects, would be no more aggressive against England now than he had shown himself in the past. If England stood aside, war with Spain was by no means inevitable; if she intervened openly and officially, it would be well-nigh certain. Even then, Burghley believed, England was well able to defend herself so long as the Spaniards did not control the coasts and ports of France.[1]

It was the collapse of the French monarchy that changed Burghley's opinion. The change began when in March 1585 the French Catholic League headed by Henry, Duke of Guise, rebelled against King Henry III and when news leaked out about the League's secret treaty of December 1584 which gave Philip II such a foothold in France as he had never had before. For now France was no longer playing, or capable of playing, its normal role as a counterpoise to Spain. The continental balance, upon which English foreign policy had usually been able to rely, no longer existed. There was now only one superpower, and that superpower was Spain. If the Dutch were now crushed, if the League, whose strength lay in those northern and northeastern parts of France nearest to England, were victorious, then all the western European coast from the Straits of Gibraltar to the estuary of the Ems would fall under Spanish control. England would then face a danger of invasion that would place an impossible burden upon her limited naval and military forces, a danger akin to that which she was later to face (though with considerably greater defensive resources) from Napoleon I and from Hitler's Germany. So, although Elizabeth clung to her old policy to the extent of again refusing the Dutch offer of the sovereignty over their countries, she did in the autumn of 1585 send Leicester, with 7,000 English troops, to their assistance.

Leicester did not exactly distinguish himself. To begin with, he

1. British Library, Harleian MSS., clxviii. fo. 102; W. Camden, *Annales*, p. 410.

infuriated the Queen by accepting the title of Governor-General from the States, an office which implied that he stood in the same relationship to her as Parma stood to Philip: the relationship of viceroy to an absentee sovereign. As Elizabeth had specifically refused the Dutch offer of their sovereignty during the negotiation of the Treaty of Nonsuch, she naturally, and accurately, regarded this as a deliberate attempt to press upon her something at the back door which she had refused at the front. Leicester also seriously exceeded the Queen's budget by taking a number of the States' troops into her pay and by a general laxness in matters of finance. Then he quarreled with the States and particularly with the province of Holland, thereby bringing the United Provinces to the verge of civil war. He even fell out with most of the Englishmen who served with and under him—with Buckhurst and Wilkes, the Norrises and Thomas Morgan.

Nevertheless, Leicester did achieve something. On the positive side, by his operations along the Ijssel, around Zutphen and Deventer, in 1586 he prevented Parma from rolling up the left flank of the Dutch defenses along the Maas and Waal in that year. Then, too, his mere presence with an army in Philip II's dominions was too open and undeniable an act of English official hostility for Philip to ignore. So Leicester was answered by the Armada. But the army of invasion that the Armada was meant to shepherd across to England was Parma's army in the Netherlands. Hence, as the Armada was originally intended for 1587 and actually came in 1588, Parma's army had to wait through those two years near the coast of Flanders instead of sweeping down the great rivers from Gelderland through Utrecht into Holland and Zeeland. Thus, when the Armada eventually arrived in the Straits of Dover, the Dutch were still in arms and Flushing and other Dutch havens were not available to Medina Sidonia for refuge and refit. Instead, after being smoked out of Calais roads by English fireships and battered off Gravelines by the Queen's galleons, he was forced to take the long and stormy way back to Spain around the north of Scotland.

Meanwhile, by encouraging the long-standing and ever-deepening enmity between Henry III and Henry of Guise, and by giving a little financial help to the Huguenots, Elizabeth had done just enough to keep France, and especially the Channel ports, from falling completely under League and Spanish domination. It was only just enough; but, as President Eisenhower once remarked, "Enough is plenty," all the more so in this case because Philip II at this stage was concerned only to neutralize France. He hesitated to act openly against the Catholic and legitimate King of France, even when Henry III, after having the Duke and Cardinal of Guise assassinated, eventually joined forces with Henry of Navarre and the Huguenots, and together they brought Paris to the verge of surrender and the League to the edge of dissolution.

In July 1589, however, Henry III was himself assassinated. That brought the Huguenot Henry of Navarre to the throne of an overwhelmingly Catholic France. The great army that had so nearly reduced Paris thereupon broke and within a few weeks the new King was in his turn virtually besieged in and around Dieppe by a revivified League. He fought his way out by defeating the Leaguers at the battle of Arques. Then with the help of English loans of money and 4,000 English troops under Lord Willoughby, he made such progress during the winter that in the spring, after Willoughby and what were left of his men had gone home, he was able to bring the League again to battle and inflict upon their army the even greater defeat of Ivry (March 1590). By July 1590 he had brought Paris once again to the verge of surrender—and once again the days of the League seemed numbered.

Thereupon Spain weighed in openly and in force. Parma, with the army from the Netherlands, marched in and relieved Paris. At the same time another 4,000 Spanish troops from Biscay landed in Brittany. The two forces, it seemed, might join hands across northern France and, although this did not in fact happen in 1590, it looked to be a very distinct possibility for 1591. In addition, the Spaniards were already talking of making Philip's daughter—the Infanta Clara Eugenia—Queen of France. The fears that had brought Elizabeth to the aid of the Dutch in 1585 seemed very likely to be realized in 1591. Accordingly the years 1591 and 1592 brought the crisis of the war and the peak of English effort on the continent, in France more especially.

This was not so by Elizabeth's intention. Like Henry VII and Henry VIII, she felt instinctively that continental jealousies would always cancel out in the long run, that Philip II's new aggressive policy would sooner or later provoke a reaction in France and in Europe and prevent him from succeeding. Elizabeth's inclination was to stand aside from the conflict except when it seemed to threaten direct and immediate danger to her own realms. She would encourage French resistance. She would exhort the German Protestant princes to raise an army to assist Henry IV; but she would not, if she could avoid it, contribute to the costs of that levy. She would encourage that army to march to France by way of the Netherlands so as to pinch Parma's troops between the Anglo-Dutch forces and the forces of Henry IV, but she did not mean to send any extra English troops to assist this operation either in the Netherlands or in France—however much her French may have misled the French ambassadors.[2]

This was a stingy but a coherent strategy. It looked at the war as a whole, from the standpoint of a supreme allied commander, as it were, and it regarded England's role as, at the most, that of an army of reserve, to be used as sparingly as possible to stop dangerous cracks in continental defenses or to exploit really attractive local opportunities for offense. Unfortunately, however, Elizabeth's allies were weak, unreliable, and all very much in the position of local area commanders, each concerned chiefly about

2. See above, p. 7.

his own local theater of operations. The German Protestants, although the Calvinist Palatinate and Hesse were now supported by the alcoholic and short-lived Lutheran Elector of Saxony, were unwilling to pay the entire cost of the levy for Henry IV and were nervous lest too great a commitment on their part against Spain and Catholicism abroad should imperil the precarious peace of the Holy Roman Empire at home. Elizabeth therefore had to contribute her £10,000, though she firmly resisted Palavicino's entreaties to go to £15,000. As for the project of bringing the German army through the Netherlands, that depended largely upon the attitude of the Dutch. And the Dutch were only concerned to use the opportunity that Parma's involvement in France gave them to clear the northeastern Netherlands provinces—Groningen and Overijssel, the vital area north of the Maas and Rhine from which their left flank could be turned. They showed very little interest in marching over the rivers through Brabant and Flanders toward the frontiers of France. So that project came to nothing.

Finally, there was Henry IV himself. His one great interest at the moment was to get as many German troops—and English troops, too, if he could—as possible as soon as possible, so that he would be able to give battle to Parma, with whom he seems to have felt a strong personal rivalry. His next major concern was to reduce Paris, the heart and soul of the League. To that end, when Parma withdrew to the Netherlands after relieving Paris in the autumn of 1590, Henry went off in the New Year to besiege Chartres. For Chartres was the chief town of a rich agricultural area that was the granary of Paris. By drawing his army down there, Henry left the coast of Normandy and the province of Brittany very poorly defended. As a result, in the spring of 1591 Elizabeth was compelled to send Sir John Norris with 3,400 English troops, later increased to 4,000, to bolster up the royalist cause in Brittany and Sir Roger Williams with another 600 to save Dieppe from the Leaguers of Rouen and Le Havre.

The danger to Dieppe was, there seems little doubt, a good deal exaggerated.[3] But just at this time, reports were coming in of mutinies among the Spanish troops in the Netherlands and that Parma was very unlikely to be able to re-enter France before, at the earliest, September. Henry IV had just taken Chartres and the moment therefore seemed opportune to try to draw him back to the Channel coast. So, as Hatton and Burghley informed Sir Roger Williams on 22 April 1591, the Queen wrote to urge the King to come back to Normandy and to besiege Rouen, offering him 3,000 or 4,000 more English troops (to be paid by him) for the purpose.[4]

The idea of besieging Rouen was not new. It went back at least to September 1589, when Henry had suggested to Ottywell Smith, an English merchant driven out of Rouen by the Leaguers and living at Dieppe, that the city of London or other English mercantile interests might make him a loan to pay his troops upon the security of repayment out of the Rouen customs after the city was captured.[5] Ottywell Smith and Aymar de Chatte, the royalist governor of Dieppe, were both enthusiastic supporters of the project, if indeed they were not its originators. And now, of course, they were vociferously supported by Sir Roger Williams, anxious to avoid serving under "Black John Norris" in Brittany.

The importance of this Dieppe lobby was that its fears and its proposals chimed in well with the ideas of influential men around the Queen. There was Williams's great friend and patron, the young Earl of Essex, who was raring to lead an English army in the field alongside the gallant Huguenot King of France. Three several times (or so he told the French ambassador, Beau-

3. H. A. Lloyd, *The Rouen Campaign 1591–1592*, pp. 64–69.
4. *List and Analysis of State Papers, Foreign Series*, II. para. 540.
5. Ibid., I. para. 480. Henry again suggested in September 1590, to Sir Edward Stafford, an attack upon Rouen if Elizabeth would send him 5,000 men paid for two months. But the suggestion was not really taken up until April 1591, by which time Henry's thoughts were moving in a rather different direction: H. A. Lloyd, *The Rouen Campaign*, pp. 37–38.

voir la Nocle) the Earl spent two hours or more on his knees before the Queen, begging her to send him to France.[6] One suspects that in the end sheer boredom at this rather ridiculous performance must have worn down her resistance!

The most powerful of all the pressures upon the Queen to take up the Dieppe lobby's suggestion came from her privy councillors. All of them had been alert, ever since Henry IV's accession, to the vital importance of keeping him and his army in the field well north of the Loire and near to the Channel coast. Only by his presence there with his main forces could the Channel provinces and Channel ports be assured against the League and Spain. The Privy Council therefore unanimously advocated the Rouen project, Burghley most of all—or so he himself said, and there seems no reason to doubt that he was telling the truth, for he repeatedly emphasized the importance of the "maritimes."[7] In fact, the only person with doubts seems to me to have been the Queen.[8] All through 1591 I get the clear impression of a united Privy Council and court pushing a hesitant and rather reluctant Queen into active intervention. By the end of June, however, she had been induced to agree to despatch Essex with 4,000 men (i.e., including Williams's 600 already at Dieppe) to Normandy to help Henry to take Rouen. But she drove a hard bargain. The men were to be paid by her for two months only; they were to be used for no operations other than the siege of Rouen; and when the city was taken the customs dues and other royal revenues there were to be handed over to her until all her loans and expenses on Henry IV's behalf since his accession had been repaid.

Essex and his troops were at Dieppe by August 1, which was reasonably quick work for sixteenth-century administration. The force was for the most part well-equipped and if the rank-and-file

6. W. B. Devereux, *Lives and Letters of the Devereux, Earls of Essex*, I.215.

7. *Correspondence of Sir Henry Unton*, p. 60.

8. Dr. Lloyd (*Rouen Campaign*, chapter IV) argues very persuasively that Elizabeth's attitude was much more positive and offensively-minded than this.

were for the most part inexperienced, they were nevertheless chosen with some care and had a fair sprinkling of veteran officers from the Netherlands wars to lead them. But they were no sooner landed than things began to go wrong, although it was not until the very end of the year that we get any hint of a break in the unanimous approval among the Queen's advisers. By that time Her Majesty's original doubts had been more than justified. To begin with, when Essex landed at Dieppe on August 1, there was no one there from the King to greet him or to inform him of the King's plans. Henry and his army, and Williams's 600 English along with them, were away besieging Noyon, on the border of Picardy. The King alleged that he went there to throw the enemy off the scent of the Rouen project while he was waiting for the English. It sounds a thin excuse,[9] and it is curious that Noyon, like Chartres, was a place in which the family of Henry's latest mistress, Gabrielle d'Estrées, had an interest. Anyway, Noyon (again like Chartres) held out much longer than had been expected and surrendered only a few days before Essex with a small escort arrived in the royal camp after a hazardous cavalcade through country infested with enemy troops. He did get Henry there to agree that, while the King himself with some horsemen went further eastward to meet his German levy now in Lorraine, the infantry of his army, under Marshal Biron, should march off back to Normandy.

Marshal Biron, however, was suffering from the gout and did not find traveling easy, so the King's infantry made no great haste to get back to Rouen. When they arrived back in Normandy, they had not got their siege train. Hence they spent three weeks mopping up small places around Rouen—Caudebec, Gournay, and so forth—places that could well have been taken earlier on, during the weeks they had spent besieging Noyon. Meanwhile, the King had gone off with his cavalry toward Sedan to meet his Ger-

9. But cf. Lloyd, *Rouen Campaign*, pp. 110–113.

man army, which had plenty of cavalry of their own to escort them (though it did perhaps need the King's personal presence to bring them to march deeper into France upon a royal promise of early payment of their wages). Certainly Henry's absence far to the east, upon the frontiers of Lorraine, made communication with him and coordination of plans very difficult and, worst of all, very slow.

Hence it was October 31, more than a month after the Queen's promised two months' pay for her troops ended, before Biron and Essex at last began to invest Rouen. It was November 13 before the King and his German levy arrived. Now, November was no time to begin a siege of a large and strong town in that part of the world. Nevertheless, the beginning of the investment, followed by the King's arrival, did encourage Elizabeth to reinforce Essex with 1,000 of her seasoned soldiers from the Netherlands and 450 pioneers. By then Essex's original 4,000 men had dwindled to less than 1,000 effectives. The siege operations, too, dragged along very slowly. It was not until December that the way up and down the Seine to Rouen was closed by English pinnaces and Dutch cromsters. Moreover, despite the urgings of English officers and some of the French council, Henry never did begin a really serious battery of either the city of Rouen or of its key Fort St. Catherine. The whole proceedings were, in fact, desultory. The skirmishes, though not infrequent, were, as Edmund Yorke remarked, "as a good base but not as a good play at football in England where men's necks, arms, and legs are broken."[10]

The fact was that all the time Henry had one eye over his shoulder, looking for Parma. He said later on, to Sir Henry Unton and Thomas Wilkes, that he had never liked the Rouen enterprise but had been induced to undertake it by the urging of some of his council.[11] There is reason to believe that this was

---

10. *List and Analysis of State Papers, Foreign Series*, III. para. 405.
11. Ibid., para. 663.

true and that his heart was never in the siege but always hankering for the chance of a pitched battle with Parma. By December that desire seemed likely soon to be gratified, for by then Parma and the Spanish army from the Netherlands were in France again and across the Somme. Accordingly, at Christmas Henry sent the Huguenot Du Plessis over to Elizabeth to seek from her yet another 5,000 English infantry, paid by her for at least six weeks. Du Plessis met with a flat refusal. During the next few months the Queen's determination to be no more involved did occasionally waver. She was now and then persuaded to think of sending, and once or twice actually to send, a little more aid, particularly when Parma, after relieving Rouen in April 1592, got into difficulties in getting back to the Netherlands.

From now onward the general trend of events made the Queen's instinctive doubts about the usefulness of anything more than purely local defensive interventions look more and more reasonable. After all, even the great Duke of Parma, although he had saved Paris in 1590 and Rouen in 1592, had been no more able to bring victory to the Catholic League than Elizabeth had been able to bring victory to the Huguenot King. Besides, coordinating operations with foreign allies had proved at least as frustrating as trying to control English commanders overseas.

By now, too, similar doubts were beginning to affect some of the Queen's advisers. As early as 6 December 1591 Burghley had written to Unton that although he was "most sorry to see the decayed estate of the King," yet "knowing how much Her Majesty is so daily charged with these foreign wars" he felt that Henry should "not press her against her mind to yield more than is convenient to her estate."[12] A few weeks later he was complaining that "if the King had attempted Rouen when he went about Noyon and those other things, afore the Duke of Parma was able to come into the field, he had won Rouen and had been able to

---

12. *Correspondence of Sir Henry Unton*, pp. 193–194.

have now at this time beaten the Duke of Parma out of France."[13] Burghley was not alone in these opinions and the doubts deepened while the number of doubters increased after Henry IV's conversion to Roman Catholicism in July 1593. The King's conversion was soon followed by the rapid collapse of the Catholic League, a collapse that was virtually complete by the summer of 1595. Paris was indeed worth a Mass.

Thus matters on the continent were getting back toward normal. Toward normal, not yet to normal, for France, even with Dutch help as well as English, was too exhausted by its long-drawn-out civil wars to be now more than a partial counterpoise to Spain. Yet at least there was no longer any danger of Spain or Spain's allies controlling the whole southern shore of the Channel. That, after all, had been the chief anxiety of Elizabeth and of Burghley, the anxiety that had pricked them into war with Spain in 1585.

If the Queen and Burghley were now beginning to draw back from involvement in the wars of the continent, there were many others among her advisers and servants who looked at the situation in a different fashion. These men—the "men of war" as opposed to the "scribes," to borrow Sir Walter Raleigh's words—saw here a chance, nay, an invitation to destroy Spanish power; in Raleigh's words once again, an invitation to have "beaten that great empire in pieces and made their kings kings of figs and oranges as in old time."[14] The chief of these, the leader of what may be called the war party, was the Earl of Essex. He had been made a privy councillor in 1593 and with the help of Anthony Bacon, the invalid brother of Francis Bacon, organized something like a rival "foreign office" to the Cecils' control of the Secretariat. Ambassadors, soldiers, sailors now wrote to him as well as to Burghley and Sir Robert Cecil, much as earlier they had corresponded with Burghley as well as with Mr. Secretary Wal-

13. Ibid., p. 293.
14. E. Edwards, *Life and Letters of Sir Walter Raleigh*, I.245.

singham. But Essex still craved a more active and martial life, and his most vociferous following was to be found among soldiers and "men of war." His growing paranoia, seeking to impose his own will upon the Queen and to monopolize counsel and patronage, turned the division of opinion over policy into a bitter personal faction fight between him and the Cecils, who were supported by the Howards. Nevertheless there was also here a genuine and fundamental difference of view about foreign policy and about the conduct of the war against Spain.

To some extent, this difference of view was one aspect of a clash of generations. *Generation*, of course, is a vague term; in a sense, one is born every minute, and even in a university there is a new one every year or two. Nevertheless, the seven or eight years following the defeat of the 1588 Spanish Armada did witness the dying off of an establishment, of an 'old gang'. In those seven or eight years there died Leicester, Walsingham, Mildmay, Croft, Hatton, Knollys, Hawkins, and Drake. In their places, a younger group was coming to the fore, young men who had grown up in the prospering Protestant 1570s and 1580s—Essex had been born in 1566. They had come to manhood in a time when France was more and more crippled by civil and religious wars, and when Spain, although the dominant Catholic power, had been partially hamstrung by the revolt of the Netherlands, by Turkish hostility, and until at least 1580 by lack of an oceangoing war navy, had seemed to them in fact to be "a colossus outward, but inwardly stuffed with clouts,"[15] a monster to be hated but not unduly feared.

For this younger generation the frustrating thing was that some of the older, less aggressive generation still hung on and still held key positions among the Queen's advisers. Burghley, born in 1520, died only in 1598. His son, Sir Robert Cecil, born in 1563 but always a very old young man, carried on his foreign policy,

15. William Herle to Burghley, 17 July 1585, S. P. Domestic, clxxx. no. 30.

with the support of Lord Admiral Howard, born in 1536, and the extensive Howard connection. Most frustrating of all was the fact that Elizabeth herself, born in 1533, belonged to that older generation which remembered the 1550s and the early 1560s, the years of Tudor England's most terrifying weakness, when the country seemed like "a bone between two dogs," when the French King bestrode the realm "having one foot in Calais and the other in Scotland," and when the King of Spain had been a necessary yet hardly less dangerous ally. Such memories made it seem particularly unwise to destroy Spanish power, even if that were feasible. For the destruction of the power of Spain might well clear the way for an even more menacing, because nearer, French overmightiness. Winning the Spanish war too decisively might well mean losing the peace that followed. To Elizabeth there was little attraction in smashing that great empire in pieces and making their kings kings of figs and oranges as in old time.

Of course, it seemed, even to Elizabeth, desirable to keep up the pressure on Spain to induce Philip to accept reasonable terms of peace. That meant, above all, restoring the Netherlands to their former unmilitarized harmlessness, under Spanish sovereignty still but freed from the presence of the Spanish army. So France was encouraged to continue the war against Spain after the downfall of the League. To this end occasional English aid was sent to Henry IV; for example, to save Brest in 1594 or after the loss of Calais to the Spaniards in 1596 or by the triple alliance of that year between England, France, and the United Provinces. It is worthy of note, however, that a secret agreement in that alliance limited the English military contribution to 2,000 men and that they were to serve only in Picardy.

In fact, after 1594 England practically withdrew from the continental war, except for the forces in the Netherlands. For the next few years the main English effort was concentrated on the naval side. Yet this still took the form largely of a privateering, commerce-destroying series of operations. The last, ill-fated expedition of Sir Francis Drake and Sir John Hawkins to the West Indies and Spanish Main in 1595–1596 was clearly of this nature. So, too, in essence was even the great Cadiz expedition of 1596, though Essex did try to make that something more. He wanted to hold Cadiz as a base for operations against Spain's naval forces and for blockading at the receiving end Spain's two most vital import traffics, the imports of silver from the mines of the New World and the imports of grain, timber, and naval stores from the Baltic lands. He received little or no support from the rest of the expedition, who were more interested in making for home with the spoils of Cadiz than in striking strategic blows at Spain's war navy and war economy. Next year he did, with Raleigh, prepare an expedition to put his project into effect.[16] For no very apparent reason, after a few setbacks from the weather and disease among his troops he abandoned the project and went off instead upon the "method of Jason" Islands voyage that failed, however, to carry away the golden, or silver, fleece. By then Tyrone's rebellion in Ireland was beginning and was to grow to proportions which for the rest of Elizabeth's reign absorbed most of the government's energies and resources, just as the French wars had done between 1589 and 1594. By 1601 England had almost 17,000 troops, horse and foot, on active service in Ireland, costing well over a quarter of a million pounds sterling a year.[17] By then, too, she no longer had France as a co-belligerent, for Henry IV had made his peace with Spain at Vervins in 1598.

All this widened the debate about the fundamentals of English foreign policy and gave it new religious and economic dimensions as well. So far as religion was concerned, English Protestants' enmity toward Spain went back, of course, at least to the time of Mary Tudor's marriage to Philip II of Spain, when even the London schoolboys pelted Philip's entourage with snowballs.

16. L. W. Henry, "Essex as a Strategist and Military Organiser, 1596–97," in *English Historical Review*, LXVIII.363–393.

17. *Somers Tracts* (ed. W. Scott, 1809), I.291–292.

But at that time it had been part of a general fear of Catholicism, of French Catholicism as well as Spanish Catholicism. The effect of the Elizabethan war with Spain and alliance with France was that, if it did not wholly take Protestant Englishmen's minds off the misdeeds of French Catholics, it did wonderfully concentrate the enmity of the more zealous upon Spain. Also, the association of Protestantism with patriotism, as well as with plunder, after the victory of 1588, did much to give Spain the first place as England's national and natural enemy.

On the economic side, the greatest influence came, inevitably, from privateering. The Spanish war after 1585 did not begin English interest in the ocean and in southward and westward trade. There had been signs of interest back in Henry VII's reign, but with the rise and growing attraction of Antwerp nearby that had proved a false dawn. In the 1530s there had been old William Hawkins's Brazil voyages and in the early 1550s those of Wyndham to West Africa. Early Elizabethan attempts to find some partial alternative to Antwerp may have given some encouragement to John Hawkins's African and Caribbean voyages in the 1560s, and the 1568–1572 quarrel gave southward and westward enterprise a further fillip in the 1570s. It was the Spanish war after 1585, however, that gave this oceanic enterprise its big push forward. The push came largely through privateering. This was increasingly organized and financed by merchants, especially by merchants of London and the south-coast ports who had been shut out of their Spanish and Portuguese markets by the war. Some of them, even before 1585, had been seeking to open new trades southward, to West Africa, to the Mediterranean, to the Levant, and in the 1580s (as with Edward Fenton's ill-fated voyage) even to the East Indies.

But it was privateering that especially drew them out in considerable numbers across the ocean to the Atlantic islands, to the West Indies, even to Virginia, and to the Pacific. It produced reasonable profits when it was run on businesslike lines and it also brought a considerable increase in English sea-power. For whereas in the Antwerp trade ships of fifty to eighty tons had been entirely adequate, on the far longer and rougher oceanic voyages there was an advantage in larger vessels carrying armaments that would enable them to tackle larger and richer prizes. Many, indeed most, of the privateers were, as we have seen, still small, still under one hundred tons. Yet whereas at Elizabeth's accession there were hardly any English-owned merchant ships larger than that, even by 1588 there were twenty-nine of over two hundred tons apiece that served against the Spanish Armada of that year.

At the same time that privateering was drawing English maritime enterprise westward and southward, the Turkish demand for armaments and the general southern-European dearth of grain increasingly opened the Mediterranean and Levant to northern shipping, English not least. These new trades, too, were reasonably rewarding. Admittedly, in total size and value they did not match the older Merchant Adventurers' and Eastland Company's trades to north Germany and the Baltic. But they were the real growth points of England's overseas commerce. They were the interest of the future, of the seventeenth century—when by the 1630s more than half of London's imports were to come from the East Indies and the Mediterranean. The men who ran them, who invested in them, were the men for whom Spain was the great obstacle almost everywhere they looked. The investors in these enterprises, moreover, were beginning to be drawn from circles beyond those of the merchant class, thanks to the development of joint-stock methods of financing.

These men, then, these interests, saw Spain as the enemy. They therefore tended to fall in behind the "war party" and, especially after about 1593, to think in terms of ocean and not of continent. They came to look upon the Spanish war as first and foremost a naval war for the domination of the seas and of maritime trade. This view was to be brilliantly amplified by a galaxy of naval historians during the late nineteenth and early twentieth centuries. It is indeed a magnificent and stirring *Westward Ho* tale, and those historians told it superbly. Yet what they wrote was very much history from the quarter-deck and it was not a little at sea. Magnificent as it was, it was not really Elizabeth's war. The real Elizabethan war with Spain was fought over the Netherlands and northern France, over western Europe not over the western hemisphere. It was this European, continental war that, together with the costly Irish rebellion from 1598 onward, imposed the heaviest and most heavily felt burdens.

The important point about those burdens is not that they made the Crown dependent upon Parliament: they did that only to a limited and temporary extent. Parliamentary taxation paid for barely half the costs of the war between 1585 and 1603 and it was not because of Elizabeth's war that the Crown debt after five years of James I's reign was more than twice what it had been after nineteen years of Elizabeth's war: £400,000 or so in 1603; over £1,000,000 in 1608. No, the important point was that to pay for the war the Elizabethan government was driven not only to increase parliamentary taxation threefold but also to resort to all kinds of desperate and burdensome expedients, to what Sir John Fortescue in the fifteenth century called "exquisite means" of taxation.[18] The sale of monopolies was the most glaring and the most resented. Patents of monopoly had always been sold with the idea of them bringing in some revenue to the Crown. But in the earlier years of Elizabeth's reign they had also had definite and clear economic motives—to foster an infant industry, or to give a new trade conditions in which it could take firm root. They had, moreover, been fairly sparingly granted. Under the pressures of war, however, they came to be more and more issued simply for the money they would bring in and upon a much wider range of commodities and activities, so wide a range that when a list

18. Sir John Fortescue, *The Governance of England* (ed. C. Plummer), chapter V.

was read out in the House of Commons in 1601 a member shouted sarcastically, "Is bread not there?"[19]

Monopolies, however, were not the only expedients of the harassed wartime government. The property of the Church, that of it which remained after the dissolution of the monasteries and chantries, was exploited and abused. The bishopric of Ely was kept without a bishop from 1581 until 1599, while the Crown kept absolute control over its revenues. When a bishop was at last installed the disadvantageous exchange of lands with the Crown which he had to make was justified by Sir Robert Cecil on the ground of the Crown's desperate need of money for the war.[20] The feudal revenues were likewise enhanced and the Court of Wards' income rose by 48 percent during the last three years of the Queen's reign. In fact, the net ordinary revenue of the Crown, that is, its revenue apart from parliamentary taxation, rose from £209,912, in the Exchequer year from Michaelmas 1571 to Michaelmas 1572, to £258,419 in 1588–1589, and to a yearly average of £326,066 between 1598 and 1603. On top of all this, between 1589 and 1603 £645,493 was raised by the sale of Crown lands,[21] a living on capital which necessarily meant some reduction of income. All this happened, too, for the most part during a time of trade depression, with many markets closed or diminished by the war; during a time, moreover, of many wet summers, poor harvests, and plague. Students of Shakespeare will remember that in the mid-1590s the London theaters were closed because of the plague.

It was resentment at these fiscal expedients that began to link anti-Spanish opinion with criticism of the government's conduct of the war and with Parliament's criticism of the burdens it imposed. During the war the government did take Parliament to a

19. J. E. Neale, *Elizabeth I and Her Parliaments, 1584–1601*, p. 380.
20. *Hist. MSS. Comm., Salisbury Papers*, XIV.114–115.
21. W. R. Scott, *English, Scottish, and Irish Joint Stock Companies*, I.96.

considerable extent into its confidence over foreign affairs. There were notable expositions by privy councillors in the House of Commons, particularly in 1593, of the war situation and the reasons for the government's need of money. The Commons were undoubtedly flattered and they seem to have had little to say upon foreign policy and strategy, apart from suggestions from privateering interests in 1589 and 1593 for a formal declaration of war against Spain, a formal declaration that, curiously, neither England nor Spain ever made. But foreign policy and strategy were continuous day-to-day matters over which a discontinuous Parliament, meeting for no more than a few weeks once in four years, could have little or no control and only a limited knowledge. On the other hand, the burdens which that policy and that strategy entailed were something that was felt continuously and daily by the members and their constituents. As a result there was a crescendo of complaint and criticism, rising from the grievances voiced in 1589 and the restrictions attempted in 1593 to the great outcry in the monopolies debates of 1601.

Underneath these storms that broke surface in Parliament there was a growing irritation among gentry and townsmen at the burdens the war imposed not only upon their purses but even more upon their time, their energy, and their patience—the burdens imposed by the levying, equipping, and arming of the 100,000 and more soldiers sent overseas during the war years, by the regular mustering and training of the countytrained bands, and by all the other extra duties directly or indirectly resulting from the war. It might appear no great hardship for the Oxford city council to give up its annual dinner and use the money to replace arms and armor lost by Oxford troops sent abroad. Nevertheless, this frequent replacement of weapons and equipment did add substantially, especially in southern counties, to the increasing burden on the local county and town rates for military matters at home and abroad. All this meant very considerable demands on local people's time and service, demands all too often accompanied by increasing badgering and interference from the central government.

It is clear that the justices of the peace, deputy lieutenants, and other local officials were growing more and more slack and grousy as the burdens mounted. The evidence for this is ample. For instance, even in 1591 the Gloucestershire troops sent with Essex to Rouen were sent off by the Gloucestershire deputy lieutenants and justices without coats.[22] We must remember, too, that it was during these war years particularly that the justices of the peace had, in Lambarde's phrase, "stacks of statutes" heaped upon them, statutes and proclamations and Privy Council directions. Most of these were due directly or indirectly to the war. There were all the orders for mustering, arming, and training the trained bands. There were poor relief and vagrancy to be dealt with on an increasing scale, especially after the 1597 and 1601 Acts of Parliament. There were Catholic recusants to be watched, and Jesuits and missionary priests from the continental seminaries to be hunted down. There were maimed and wounded soldiers to be provided for, especially after the 1593 Act. There was particular care about the corn trade during the years of dearth and wet harvests. Small wonder if justices of the peace and other local officials grumbled and dragged their feet.

Nor was service overseas much more popular among the lower orders of Elizabethan society who made up the rank-and-file of continental expeditionary forces. Their feelings were perhaps voiced for them by Sir John Smith in his famous invocation of Magna Carta against impressment for service out of the country, even though his protest came after a very good lunch at the Essex county musters and he was, by his own admission, very drunk at the time. The rank-and-file, however, for the most part voted with their feet. Desertion was endemic and mutiny not unknown among levies for overseas service. Essex drafts, possibly encour-

22. *List and Analysis of State Papers, Foreign Series*, III. para. 256.

aged by Sir John Smith's tipsy harangue, mutinied in the 1590s. In late 1592, out of 1,300 men from southern counties levied by Sir John Norris for service in Brittany, 600 deserted before they left their ports of embarkation in England.[23] Prospects of survival, after all, were small and the chances of keeping in touch with home, even for those who could write, were very slender, as the tale of Ralph Damport in Thomas Dekker's *Shoemaker's Holiday* illustrates. Many, indeed, of those pressed for service in France or the Netherlands must have echoed the soldier in Shakespeare's *Henry* V: "Would I were in an alehouse in London. I would give all my fame for a pot of ale and safety."

What made it all so exceedingly frustrating was that the war dragged on for nineteen long years and that, although victory seemed on several occasions—in 1589, in 1591, in 1596—just around the corner, in the event it never arrived. On those three occasions victory did seem almost within sight, at least victory in the sense that Elizabeth understood it: the expulsion of Spanish troops from the Netherlands and those countries' return to the substantial measure of home rule they had enjoyed under Charles V, combined with the restoration of the French monarchy to strength and independence as an effective counterpoise to Spanish mightiness. On each occasion, however, victory slipped away. Those whose shoulders were most galled by the burdens therefore tended to blame the government, some for not making peace, quite as many for not winning the war. This happened all the more because government and administration were during these last years of the reign getting considerably more inbred, and court and country were beginning to grow apart. All this added up to a widespread groundswell of grumbling, to much dragging of the feet, to a great deal of local irritation. It all bred a new and more critical attitude to the central government, to the monarchy itself, even to the monarch personally. Few went so far

23. S. P. France (S.P.78), xxx. fo. 15.

as Essex, who once in a fit of petulance burst out that the old Queen's mind was become as crooked as her carcase.[24] Indeed, let us not exaggerate. The Spanish war at the close of the sixteenth century did not cause the English civil war of the mid-seventeenth century. A lot happened in between, including James I and Charles I. But the Elizabethan war with Spain and the long-drawn-out burdens it imposed did play a considerable part in changing sixteenth-century Englishmen from a king-worshipping nation into a king-criticizing nation.

Furthermore, growing numbers began to link criticism of the government with an anti-Spanish view about foreign policy and this linkage grew closer as the seventeenth century wore on. Thus when in 1604 James I made peace with Spain, the news was greeted with an ominous silence in London and eight years later the Venetian ambassador said that the mass of both nobles and people desired war with Spain.[25] James I's Spanish marriage policy was a major cause of his people's mistrust, and while Sir John Eliot spoke of an Anglo-French alliance as natural, Sir John Oglander looked back regretfully to Elizabeth's reign when "we had in a good manner wars with Spain and peace with France" under a Queen in whom "there was nothing wanting that could be desired in a prince but that she was a woman."[26] By the middle of the seventeenth century, criticism of the government and anti-Spanish views on foreign policy had become so closely identified that the overthrow of the monarchy meant that, as Oliver Cromwell put it, "Truly your great enemy is the Spaniard."

24. W. B. Devereux, *Lives of the Devereux, Earls of Essex*, II.131.

25. S. R. Gardiner, *History of England*, I.214; *Calendar of State Papers, Venetian, 1607–10*, p. 101.

26. *A Royalist's Notebook* (ed. F. Bamford), pp. 49, 192.

Epilogue

The effects of the Elizabethan war with Spain upon English foreign policy were much wider and much longer-lasting than the comparatively brief official triumph of the anti-Spanish view under Oliver Cromwell. The Elizabethan quarrels with Spain, by drawing Englishmen out to and across the oceans, had added a new dimension to English policy. Till then its horizons had been virtually limited to the Netherlands—Antwerp in particular—and northern France, with decidedly secondary and mainly commercial interests in northern Germany and the Baltic and in the Bordeaux wine trade. These nearer continental interests were still liable to become dominant at times, but now only when the balance between the greater powers of Europe was again destroyed and one or other of them became threateningly overmighty, as Louis XIV's France did after the dramatic collapse of Spanish power in the 1667 War of Devolution, or as Napoleon I's France did, or Adolf Hitler's Germany.

At other times England more or less turned its back on the continent, though with fairly frequent glances over its shoulder to encourage the continental nations to independence or (if you prefer) to stay divided in a state of mutual balance. Ideally, the balance was to be kept steady enough to promise reasonable permanence, yet sufficiently insecure to keep the balancing powers jealously eying one another and to prevent them attempting to follow England too vigorously across the oceans.

As a result, so long as England kept up its sea-power, it could generally forget those fears of continental invasion, of continental domination, that had haunted it since the loss of its medieval kings' French possessions and while Scotland remained hostile and Ireland unsubdued. Now there would be serious danger only if one single power were allowed to grow overmighty on the continent of Europe. So there was built into English foreign policy a duality of ocean and continent. In normal, peaceful times the dominant influence, the dominant attraction, was that of the ocean. In times of European crisis, when the continental balance was upset, the influence of the continent was the more powerful, as questions of home defense came uppermost in Englishmen's thoughts.

This duality of ocean and continent remained at the heart of English foreign policy until in the twentieth century the development of air-power and of still more infernal engines of war once again deprived England of the defense of insularity and its shield of sea-power. These developments also made wide, ocean-linked possessions untenable. Yet it still left the English people with a nostalgia for the old oceanic ways, torn between ocean and continent, a people who "have lost an empire and have not yet found a role."

Suggestions For
Further Reading

J. A. Froude's *History of England from the Fall of Wolsey to the Defeat of the Armada* (1st ed., 1856–70; Longmans; numerous later editions) has its faults and is over one hundred years old, but still in its final seven volumes gives one of the best, fullest, and liveliest accounts of Elizabeth's policy before 1588. The second half of R. B. Wernham's *Before the Armada: The Growth of English Foreign Policy 1485–1588* (1966; Cape; Norton paperback ed., 1972) deals more compactly with the same period. E. P. Cheyney's *History of England from the Defeat of the Armada to the Death of Elizabeth* (2 vols., 1914 and 1926; Longmans) is the fullest, though not entirely adequate, account of Elizabethan policy and institutions after 1588. The first volume of Sir John Seeley's *Growth of British Policy 1558–1688* (2nd ed., 1897; Cambridge U.P.) is a brilliant but not wholly accurate study. Conyers Read's books on *Mr. Secretary Cecil and Queen Elizabeth* (1955; Cape), *Lord Burghley and Queen Elizabeth* (1960; Cape), and *Mr. Secretary Walsingham and the Policy of Queen Elizabeth* (3 vols., 1925; Clarendon Press, Oxford) are almost as full as Froude and more balanced, though much less lively. A. L. Rowse's *Expansion of Elizabethan England* (1955; Macmillan) is also useful on some aspects. The best textbook is J. B. Black's *Reign of Elizabeth* in the Oxford History of England (2nd ed., 1959; Clarendon Press, Oxford). J. E. Neale's *Queen Elizabeth* (1934; Cape; numerous editions since) is the most satisfactory life of the Queen. J. Hurstfield's *Queen Elizabeth and the Unity of England* (1960; "Teach Yourself History," English Universities Press) is a notable short sketch.

On particular aspects of policy H. Lloyd's *Rouen Campaign 1590–1592*

(1973; Clarendon Press, Oxford) is excellent. C. Wilson discusses *Queen Elizabeth and the Revolt of the Netherlands* (1970; Macmillan).

On naval affairs Sir Julian Corbett's *Drake and the Tudor Navy* (2 vols., 2nd ed., 1899; Longmans) and his *Successors of Drake* (1900; Longmans) are the fullest accounts. J. A. Williamson's *John Hawkins* (1927; Clarendon Press, Oxford. Revised ed., 1949) and his *Age of Drake* (1938; Black) are important. K. R. Andrews's *Drake's Voyages* (1967; Weidenfeld and Nicolson) is a brief masterpiece and his *Elizabethan Privateering* (1964; Cambridge U.P.) is also important. On the Armada of 1588 G. Mattingly's *Defeat of the Spanish Armada* (1959; Cape) is a superb study of the campaign and its European background. M. Lewis's *Spanish Armada* (1960; Batsford) and I. A. A. Thompson's article on 'Armada Guns' in *Mariners Mirror*, LXI (1975): 355–71 are also important. Two books on military matters call for mention—L. O. J. Boynton's *Elizabethan Militia 1558–1640* (1967; Routledge and Kegan Paul), and for overseas expeditions and their organization C. G. Cruickshank's *Elizabeth's Army* (2nd ed., 1966; Clarendon Press, Oxford).

On government and administration, besides the chapters in Cheyney (above), there is an excellent brief study in A. G. R. Smith's *Government of Elizabethan England* (1967; Edward Arnold). F. M. G. Evans's *The Principal Secretary 1558–1688* (1923; Manchester U.P.) is the standard account of that office. W. MacCaffrey's *Shaping of the Elizabethan Regime* (1968; Princeton U.P.; 1969; Cape) is a valuable survey of the first ten years of the reign. G. R. Elton's "Tudor Government: Points of Contact" in *Transactions of the Royal Historical Society*, 5th series, XXIV (1974): 159–82, XXV (1975): 195–211, and XXVI (1976): 211–28; E. W. Ives's *Faction in Tudor England* (1979; Historical Association Appreciations in History, no. 6); and J. E. Neale's "Elizabethan Political Scene" (British Academy Raleigh Lecture, 1948, reprinted in *Essays in Elizabethan History*, 1958; Cape) have useful insights. J. E. Neale's *Queen Elizabeth and her Parliaments* (2 vols., 1953 and 1957; Cape) is the standard account of parliamentary affairs. The most useful works on government finance are F. C. Dietz's *English Public Finance 1558–1641* (1932; Century Co., New York) and W. R. Scott's *English, Scottish, and Irish Joint Stock Companies to 1720* (1912; Cambridge U.P.).

For overseas trade, besides the chapters in Cheyney (above), there is a good brief account in R. Davis's *English Overseas Trade 1500–1700* (1973; Macmillan) and a fuller one in G. D. Ramsay's *English Overseas Trade in the Centuries of Emergence* (1957; Macmillan). Ramsay's *City of London in International Affairs at the Accession of Elizabeth Tudor*

(1975; Manchester U.P.) is valuable for the early stage of the first quarrel with Spain, for which E. E. Rich's introduction to the *Ordinance Book of the Merchants of the Staple* (1937; Cambridge U.P.) is also useful.

On the continental background J. H. Elliott's *Europe Divided 1559–1598* (1968; Collins, "Fontana") is the best concise account. There is also the *New Cambridge Modern History*, volume III (ed. R. B. Wernham; 1968; Cambridge U.P.). See, too, G. Mattingly's brilliant *Renaissance Diplomacy* (1955; Cape). For Spain the best textbook is J. Lynch's *Spain under the Habsburgs*, volume I (1964; Blackwell, Oxford); I. A. A. Thompson's *War and Government in Habsburg Spain 1560–1620* (1976; Athlone Press) and P. O'M. Pierson's *Philip II* (1975; Thames and Hudson) are also valuable. For France there are J. Salmon's *Society in Crisis: France in the Sixteenth Century* (1975; Ernest Benn); R. Briggs's *Early Modern France 1560–1715* (1977; Oxford U.P.); and N. M. Sutherland's *Massacre of St. Bartholomew and the European Conflict 1559–1572* (1973; Macmillan). On the Netherlands the outstanding work is P. Geyl's *Revolt of the Netherlands* (1932; Williams and Norgate); see also G. Parker's *Dutch Revolt, 1548–1648* (1977; Allen Lane) and his *Army of Flanders and the Spanish Road 1567–1659* (1972; Cambridge U.P.).

Penry Williams's *Tudor Regime* (1979: Clarendon Press, Oxford) appeared after this book was in the press.

Index

Index

Compositor: Graphic Composition
Printer: Thomson-Shore
Binder: Thomson-Shore
Text: Linotron 202 Electra
Display: Linotron 202 Bembo